BECOMING MORE LIKE JESUS
THROUGH THE PRAYER OF ST. FRANCIS

Make Me an Instrument of Your Peace

MARK DEYMAZ

NavPress

Published in alliance with Tyndale House Publishers

NavPress
Bold. Loving. Sensible.

NavPress.com

Make Me an Instrument of Your Peace: Becoming More like Jesus Through the Prayer of St. Francis

A NavPress resource published in alliance with Tyndale House Publishers

The Team:
David Zimmerman, Publisher; Deborah Sáenz, Acquisitions Editor; Andrew Pottenger, Copyeditor; Lacie Phillips, Production Assistant; Sarah Susan Richardson, Cover Designer, Brandi Davis, Interior Designer

For information about special discounts for bulk purchases, please contact Tyndale House Publishers at csresponse@tyndale.com, or call 1-855-277-9400.

ISBN 979-8-89802-017-0

Printed in the United States of America

32 31 30 29 28 27 26
7 6 5 4 3 2 1

In this world of chaos, conflict, and confusion, now is the hour for us all to beat our swords into plowshares and do the demanding work of Christian peacemaking. Mark DeYmaz shows us how to use St. Francis's Peace Prayer to sow seeds of love, hope, and joy and thereby to align ourselves with Christ's amazing mission of peace. This is a challenging book but also a necessary book for these calamitous times.

MICHAEL FROST, Morling College, author of *Surprise the World*

This book is Isaiah 61 with skin on—turning ashes into beauty, despair into hope, and readers into reconcilers. Mark DeYmaz doesn't just write about peace—he hands you the tools to make it.

LEONARD SWEET, author, professor, preacher, publisher, and proprietor

The beloved Prayer of St. Francis is as important today as it has been for decades. More than ever, we need to pray that God will help us manifest the love of Jesus in our troubled world. Mark DeYmaz draws from his own life, as well as his years of ministry, to help us do that.

ALICE FRYLING, spiritual director and author of *Aging Faithfully*

Post-Christian, anti-Christian, deconstructed Christian, red states/blue states, nationalism, anger, division, war. In a deeply segmented world with seemingly growing anger toward Christianity, we need a way forward. *Make Me an Instrument of Your Peace* is that way forward, a wonderful call for us to focus on the Prince of Peace and demonstrate that peace to a hungry world. This is the Christian witness. Organizing how to practice peace through the Prayer of St. Francis, Mark DeYmaz expertly and clearly guides us to reorient ourselves to draw people to Christ, seek reconciliation, pursue unity, and heal our land.

DR. MICHAEL O. EMERSON, Rice University, author of *Divided by Faith* and *Kingdom Racial Change*

For those who feel life is heavy or whose faith feels shaky, Mark's book offers gentle steps back toward hope and light. As Christ followers unite around the truths of the Peace Prayer, we'll see the movement of Jesus bring a glimpse of heaven to earth.

KRISTIN MOCKLER YOUNG, teaching pastor at Mosaic Church and host of *The Becoming Church Podcast*

Mark weaves together his own ministerial and fatherly journey with the pastoral heart of St. Francis's prayer. Like one working with the shards of a stained glass window, Mark situates the joys and struggles and everything in between from years of ministerial insight into a book that will shine brightly for anyone who reads it, but especially for Christians seeking to know the Lord's will in their lives. As a Catholic priest, I gained insight from it and will recommend it wholeheartedly to others.

FR. JOSEPH DE ORBEGOZO, priest of the Diocese of Little Rock

Dr. DeYmaz is widely recognized for his work in spaces of multiracial ministry and church economics. In his latest book, he utilizes the Peace Prayer to encourage effective Christian witness and ministry in an increasingly secular society. *Make Me an Instrument of Your Peace* is both inspirational and practical, showing us how to become more like Jesus and less like the world in ways that draw others to Christ. It shows us a path to true peacemaking.

DR. GEORGE YANCEY, professor of sociology at Baylor University

Mark DeYmaz has written a timely book for anyone longing to follow Jesus more faithfully in a world of conflict. Rooted in the wisdom of the Prayer of St. Francis, a prayer I pray every day, this book masterfully guides us toward becoming people of peace. Mark invites us to love, offer hope, and bring joy to our neighborhoods, which are filled with hidden hate, despair, and quiet sadness. *Make Me an Instrument of Your Peace* will encourage your heart and challenge your priorities, pointing you toward the Spirit's work of inner transformation that prompts reconciliation and justice in God's good world.

DEREK VREELAND, pastor and author of the God in the Neighborhood Bible Studies

Mark DeYmaz has written a book that brings theology down to the street level—where division, exhaustion, and cynicism too often reign. *Make Me an Instrument of Your Peace* isn't sentimental spirituality; it's a manual for people who want to practice the way of Jesus in a world that's forgotten how he lived.

DR. TERRY CRIST, colead pastor at City of Grace and author of *Loving Samaritans*

Make Me an Instrument of Your Peace challenges the church to move beyond rhetoric and embody the reconciling love of Christ in a world yearning for care. DeYmaz calls us to follow Jesus into the hard work of reconciliation, reminding us that lasting peace is born not of avoidance but of love expressed through daily grace.

REV. DR. CHRISTOPHER J. BENEK, pastor at First Miami Presbyterian Church and CEO of CoCreators

As a first-generation immigrant and minister, I've walked the tightrope between cultures and faith, and I know how desperately our world needs peacemakers who don't just talk about peace but also live it. With depth, humility, and clarity, Dr. Mark DeYmaz invites us to become living conduits of God's love for all, seeing and valuing others through his lens.

DR. SAEHEE DURAN, ordained minister of the Assemblies of God USA

If you're a Christian ready to live boldly for Christ in a world that often rejects him, *Make Me an Instrument of Your Peace* is a must-read. This book is a powerful call to be Christlike in the face of hostility, to embody the hope the world desperately needs that is too often misrepresented by Christians. It challenges believers to become credible witnesses to the gospel, reflecting the beauty of the greatest love story ever told. Let the world see Jesus through our good works.

COREEN ESPLIN, Tonawanda Seneca, dean of women at Indigenous Bible College

In *Make Me an Instrument of Your Peace*, Mark draws our hearts to remember the power of peace—peace as a sign and wonder and as evidence of a mature faith—so that our witness of love might stand as a prophetic contrast amid the prevailing narratives of hostility. When alienation and contempt seem the easier paths, the vocation of the peacemaker summons us to the transcendent way of Christ—a way not conformed to this world. In such faithful embodiment, the hope of the gospel finds its most compelling expression.

NOEMI CHAVEZ, lead pastor at Revive Church

Christians are uniquely called to follow the way of Jesus, the Prince of Peace. Yet in our contentious world, peacemaking often seems more like an elusive goal than an attainable reality. In *Make Me an Instrument of Your Peace*, Mark DeYmaz guides us to a path he also walks, moving beyond words to do the hard and sacrificial work of making peace. I pray heaven is pleased with the glorious sound that flows from hands and hearts yielded as instruments of peace.

DORENA WILLIAMSON, bestselling author and associate pastor of belonging at Strong Tower Bible Church

Even with its challenge about sin, the gospel is ultimately about an invitation to connect with God and the hope that relationship brings to life. That means our engagement must be inviting, not just challenging. *Make Me an Instrument of Your Peace* is a powerful reminder that how we engage is as important—if not more so—than seeking to be right. This book aims at the heart through a prayer for being peaceful yet true. Biblical engagement must be true and yet reflect the heart of God to reach those who need him. In an era when this balance is often missing, this book is a godsend. In short, tone matters because posture is as important as position.

DR. DARRELL L. BOCK, executive director for cultural engagement at the Hendricks Center and senior research professor of New Testament studies at Dallas Theological Seminary

This book is different from Mark's previous works. This is not Mark the leader speaking to other church leaders. It is Mark the pastor speaking to laity and clergy alike about what it means to be people who make peace and are an effective witness in our day. Mark does not merely rely on his own wisdom. He uses the famous Prayer of St. Francis to guide us into and out of many of the anxieties, fears, and doubts of the present moment, showing how Jesus is still the solution to what ails our broken world.

ESAU McCAULLEY, PHD, Jonathan Blanchard Associate Professor of New Testament and Public Theology at Wheaton College and author of *How Far to the Promised Land*

To Linda, who was the first to dream with me of planting a church for all people, on earth as it is in heaven; to our adult children, Zack, Emily, Will, and Kate, who supported the endeavor sacrificially; and to our grandchildren, Grace, Catherine, Pierce, Sicilia, Ford, and Sterling.

Matthew 5:9

Contents

Peace Prayer

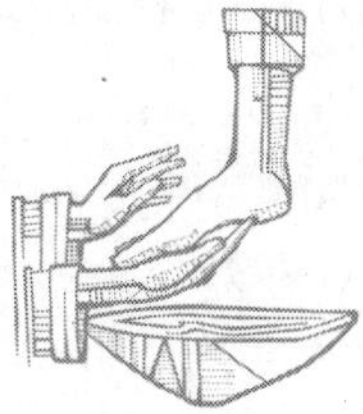

COMMON ENGLISH

Lord, make me an instrument of your peace:
where there is hatred, let me sow love;
where there is injury, pardon;
where there is doubt, faith;
where there is despair, hope;
where there is darkness, light;
where there is sadness, joy.

O divine Master, grant that I may not so much seek
to be consoled as to console,
to be understood as to understand,
to be loved as to love.
For it is in giving that we receive,
it is in pardoning that we are pardoned,
and it is in dying that we are born to eternal life.

ORIGINAL FRENCH

Seigneur, faites de moi un instrument de votre paix.
Là où il y a de la haine, que je mette l'amour.
Là où il y a l'offense, que je mette le pardon.
Là où il y a la discorde, que je mette l'union.
Là où il y a l'erreur, que je mette la vérité.
Là où il y a le doute, que je mette la foi.
Là où il y a le désespoir, que je mette l'espérance.
Là où il y a les ténèbres, que je mette votre lumière.
Là où il y a la tristesse, que je mette la joie.

Ô Maître, que je ne cherché pas tant
À être console qu'à consoler,
À être compris qu'à comprendre
À être aimé qu'à aimer.
Car c'est en donnant qu'on reçoit,
C'est en s'oubliant qu'on trouve,
C'est en pardonnant qu'on est pardonné,
C'est en mourant qu'on ressuscite à l'éternelle vie.

LITERAL ENGLISH

Lord, make me an instrument of your peace.
Where there is hatred, that I may put love.
Where there is offense, that I may put pardon.
Where there is discord, that I may put union.
Where there is error, that I may put the truth.
Where there is doubt, that I may put faith.
Where there is despair, that I may put hope.
Where there is darkness, that I may put your light.
Where there is sadness, that I may put joy.

O Master, that I may not so much seek
to be consoled as to console,
to be understood as to understand,
to be loved as to love.
For it is in giving that one receives,
it is in forgetting oneself that one finds,
it is in forgiving that one is forgiven,
it is in dying that one is reborn to eternal life.

PART 1

Anointed with Christ

CHAPTER 1

Represent Jesus Well

From Issachar, [people] who understood
the times and knew what Israel should do.

1 CHRONICLES 12:32

In December 2022, the first Jesus Now Summit was held in Dallas, Texas. Hosted by the Barna Group in partnership with several other influential organizations, about one hundred ministry leaders gathered to consider the why, how, and what behind the recently launched *He Gets Us* campaign.[1]

As we learned, the campaign was created to address a single sobering question: How did the world's greatest love story become associated with hate?[2] Or, to ask it differently, why do some people view Christians as part of a hate group?

At the gathering, David Kinnaman (Barna's CEO) and Jason Vanderground (president of BrandHaven) shared findings from a study conducted between April and July 2021 that helped shape the campaign.[3] The data revealed that 80 percent of US adults are "somewhat certain" or "completely certain" that Jesus existed about two thousand years ago.[4] Even among "spiritually open" skeptics, 42 percent have a favorable view of him.[5] Many believe that Jesus is

- *inclusive:* He's for everyone.
- *positive:* His teachings are good for society as a whole.
- *exemplary:* He provides a worthy example by which to live . . . he loves us all.[6]

The research also revealed that most adults in the United States are familiar with Christianity, the Bible, and Jesus. Additionally, 50 percent of adults—especially those raising children—are open to learning more about Jesus and can be reached by meeting their felt or holistic needs.[7] This was not only surprising but encouraging.

But when Kinnaman shared additional findings from October 2022, the tone in the room shifted. As he reported, nearly half of US adults—47 percent—say they've had experiences that led them to "deconstruct or take apart the faith of [their] youth."[8] Similarly, 48 percent of Gen Z report disillusionment with their experiences in Christian churches.[9]

AVOID MISREPRESENTATION

Broadly speaking, the studies show that while many Americans have confidence in Jesus, they do not trust Christians or the church, which they perceive as failing to reflect the spirit of the biblical Christ.

This disconnect is especially evident among spiritually open skeptics, who reject the hypocrisy, judgmentalism, and discrimination they associate with scandals and controversies plaguing churches.[10] As a result, many are unwilling to hear from Christians and tend to resist Christian messaging.[11]

Many also struggle to recognize—or even outright reject—Jesus' divinity and the concept of having a personal relationship with him. Therefore, statements that attempt to defend or promote Christianity often prove ineffective. That's why *He Gets Us* was launched: to raise the respect for and relevance of Jesus—and to call Christians to best reflect his love in their interactions with others.[12]

Whether through perception or lived experience, many today believe Christians do not speak, act, or live like Jesus. Likewise, they tend to view Christians as self-serving—at odds with the apostle Paul's instruction: "In humility value others above yourselves, not looking to your own interests but each of you to the interests of the others" (Philippians 2:3-4).

These insights aren't just interesting—they invite our full attention. Understanding the times in which we live helps us confront reality with honesty and respond with intentionality. If Christians are perceived by many as a hate group, our credibility and our witness are at risk. And if people don't like or trust those who claim to follow Christ, why would they be open to the gospel at all?

EXAMINE ASSUMPTIONS

In the twentieth century, Christians were taught to explain biblical truth logically to non-Christians and defend our faith through the practice of modern apologetics. Evangelization took place at what Kinnaman referred to as "the bridge of Christ's divinity."[13] For example:

- We brought preachers like Billy Graham and Luis Palau to our cities. With heartfelt words and a compelling argument, these and others like them spoke divine truth about Jesus, and people responded by coming forward in the moment to repent of sin and put their faith in him.

- We initiated conversations with others door to door, on a plane, or at the beach, asking, "Do you know for sure that if you died tonight, you would go to heaven?" In those days, people were typically receptive, rarely impolite, and often responsive to the Holy Spirit as we explained the Four Spiritual Laws, the "Romans Road," or other presentations of the gospel.[14]
- We passed out copies of Josh McDowell's *Evidence That Demands a Verdict*, G. K. Chesterton's *The Everlasting Man*, and later, *The Case for Christ* by Lee Strobel. These books and others like them presented biblical truth, historical facts, and a clear rationale for the Christian faith which resonated positively with readers.

Yet times have changed. Non-Christian adults are no longer inclined or receptive to Christianity. Furthermore, they see Christians as hypocritical, judgmental, and discriminatory. Their perceptions about us turn them off and make them mad.

SHIFT PERCEPTIONS

In the twenty-first century, then, what we say about Jesus means very little to others apart from tangible action that represents him well. For this reason, I believe we're living in a Matthew 5:16 century.[15]

In this passage, Jesus does not say, "Let them hear your good words." Instead, he says, "Let them see your good works. That's what will compel them toward your Father in heaven" (paraphrase mine).

So it is today. People are drawn more to what they see Christians doing with joy, faithfulness, and authenticity than to what they hear us saying. Practical engagement through acts of kindness and generosity—rooted in empathy—are better starting points for eventual conversations with others about life, meaning, and their eternal future. Yes, there are many ways to speak about Jesus. Explanation is good; but these days, demonstration is better.

In order to reverse the decline of trust in Christians and the church, it's wise to first engage spiritually open skeptics or wounded cynics "at the bridge of Christ's humanity"—meeting them where they are with kindness and good works—before attempting to speak of his divine nature. By quietly advancing the common good, we offer a credible witness to the gospel without saying a word. In doing so, we help shift negative perceptions, dismantle skepticism, and patiently lead others toward "the bridge of Christ's divinity," where they can encounter Jesus, explore biblical truth, and ultimately, as we hope, choose to follow him.

To be clear, God's mission to restore and reconcile people to himself by means of Christ's redemptive work remains the same throughout time. So does his expectation that followers will actively share their faith in Jesus with others. Nevertheless, our approach needs to change if we are to help those in our day "believe that he exists and that he rewards those who earnestly seek him" (Hebrews 11:6).

PROVIDE A COMPELLING WITNESS

In a world marked by conflict, violence, and hatred, it's long past time for Christians to identify with Christ as peacemakers

(Matthew 5:9). Indeed, we are uniquely called, equipped, and expected by God to advance peace on earth rather than to hinder it.

Peace can be understood as a state of reconciliation, harmony, and wholeness—both within oneself and in relationships with others. It's marked by the presence of love and justice, and the absence of conflict or division. Peace actively pursues unity and healing in the face of brokenness.

If it's true—as research suggests—that the world's greatest love story has become associated with hate, then we should ask ourselves:

- *How can I become a more compelling witness of God's grace, mercy, and compassion?*
- *What attitudes should I adopt or abandon to better reflect Jesus before others?*
- *How might I recognize others' pain to help them experience healing and peace?*

One day, while reflecting on such questions, I recalled a prayer that was introduced to me at an early age. The Prayer of St. Francis, also called the Peace Prayer, has been recited by people throughout the world for more than one hundred years. Published in the early twentieth century, the prayer provides petitioners with noble guidance, serving as both a moral and spiritual compass for interaction with others.

The Peace Prayer is a recipe for how to be identified with Jesus and become more like him. By applying its precepts, we can sow seeds of love, pardon, faith, hope, light, joy, and understanding in the lives of others we encounter on a daily basis. In so doing, we can align with Christ on a mission of peace.[16]

To be clear, I didn't write this book as someone who has fully mastered peacemaking, but as someone still on a journey—hoping to help you become part of the solution to the hurt, polarization, and animosity that continue to plague our world. By practicing the Peace Prayer, we can become more like Jesus in these divisive times. If, as is often said, "we are his hands and feet" or "the only Jesus some will ever see," then for each of us the question becomes: *How can I best represent him in a world of chaos, conflict, and confusion?*

KEEP GOING

Beyond our own shifts in attitudes and approaches to evangelization, entire congregations should address these questions for the same reason. For instance, it's admirable that churches send people and money across oceans to address the physical, material, and spiritual needs of others without Christ. Yet entire communities in our own country wonder why the same energy and effort is not put forth to address the similar needs of people living across the street. Where this is true, the credibility of our collective witness is undermined, and it keeps our neighbors from trusting the church.

I once coached a group of North Carolina pastors and loaded them into a fifteen-passenger van to tour the local area. Specifically, I wanted them to look with fresh eyes upon the community and to see people beyond church walls. Leaving the church parking lot, I drove the van to an apartment complex across the street. While we were getting a feel for the place and its residents, a young woman, seemingly in her twenties, came out of an apartment to walk a dog. Pulling alongside her, I rolled down the window and explained that we were pastors touring the community to learn more about it.

I asked, "What can you tell us about the church across the street?"

"What church?" she replied without hesitation, leaving the pastors speechless.

Now imagine this young woman getting into a car every morning and leaving for work or school; and there, right in front of her, is a church. There's even a sign with the church's name on it along with other identifying information. Yet she's never noticed the church. She doesn't even know it's there.

By contrast, a prominent advocate for inadequately sheltered and homeless people in our city recently came to our church to get a wheelchair—one specifically designed for individuals missing limbs. Having long ago "deconstructed" his faith, this man in his early forties shared that he had not been actively involved with Christianity or a church for years. One of our members then showed him around the building. It's a one-hundred-thousand-square-foot former Kmart that now houses shower and laundry facilities for the urban poor; a fully staffed medical clinic providing primary care, mental health, and social services to people without insurance; a community counseling clinic; a fitness gym; and more. When the tour ended, the man asked, "Where's the church?"—affirming both our approach and its outcomes. I thanked him for what, in that moment, was one of the greatest compliments our church had ever received. Later, he shared about his experience on Facebook, saying, "I left church a lot of years ago because I just couldn't find one 'doing it' anywhere or willing to equip me to do it. Friday, I saw a church DOING IT no matter what anyone says or thinks. So impressed and grateful, Mosaic. Please, keep going!!"[17] Both his comment and subsequent post affirmed that we were representing Jesus well in our community—through good works and by pointing others to the cross, as we continue to do today.

Becoming instruments of peace opens the door to engage both the wounded and the wondering—those hurt by the church and those unsure about Christ. In so doing, we can represent Jesus in ways that are credible, meaningful, and relatable. Even more, our lives will inspire others and point them to "the bridge of Christ's divinity" where Jesus offers forgiveness, reconciliation with God, and everlasting life.

Ultimately, that's what this book is all about.

QUESTIONS FOR REFLECTION

1. Does the *He Gets Us* research match your own experience or perceptions about how others view Christians or the church? If so, how?
2. What can we do to address the problem, promote promising solutions, and change the narrative where Christians and the church are concerned?
3. Do you know anyone currently struggling with challenging concerns or circumstances? What can you do to meet them at the bridge of Christ's humanity, leading with works rather than words?

CHAPTER 2

Reflect His Anointing

I was born in San Francisco, California, in 1961 and raised in Alameda as the only child in a single-parent home. Since my mother, Dorothy, converted to Catholicism as an adult, I grew up attending Mass at St. Joseph's Basilica on Sunday mornings. In 1971, we moved to Phoenix, Arizona, just before the start of my sixth-grade year. A year later, I transferred from a public middle school—where the primary spring sport was softball—to St. Gregory Catholic School, where the boys played baseball. We began attending "St. Greg's" too, where at the church I became an altar server and worked weeknights in the rectory answering phones.[1]

Upon graduation from junior high, I was enrolled at Brophy College Preparatory, a private Jesuit school that educates "ninth through twelfth grade 'Men for Others to Serve the World' and form young men who are intellectually competent, open to growth, religious, loving, and committed to doing justice."[2] There, I began working in a different rectory—this one housing some twenty-five

Jesuit priests and novitiates.[3] As part of Brophy's work-scholarship program, my duties included monitoring the switchboard, setting tables, and serving dinner.

When my mother and I moved to Scottsdale, we began attending a Protestant church with a vibrant student ministry in the fall of 1981. As a college freshman, it was here that I committed myself to more passionately pursuing Christ by faith.[4] Three years later, having earned a bachelor of science degree in psychology, I entered full-time ministry as a youth pastor.

Through my experiences as a Catholic, I was taught to memorize and recite the Prayer of St. Francis—the Peace Prayer. Yet after serving in Protestant churches for more than forty years, I've observed that this prayer is not as often referenced or discussed. Still, I believe that if internalized, this beautiful recitation can have a transformative impact on our mindset, behavior, and spiritual life.

As commonly translated in English, the Peace Prayer reads:

Lord, make me an instrument of your peace:
where there is hatred, let me sow love;
where there is injury, pardon;
where there is doubt, faith;
where there is despair, hope;
where there is darkness, light;
where there is sadness, joy.

O divine Master, grant that I may not so much seek
to be consoled as to console,
to be understood as to understand,
to be loved as to love.

For it is in giving that we receive,
it is in pardoning that we are pardoned,
and it is in dying that we are born to eternal life.[5]

DISCOVER THE ORIGIN

Since the First World War, the Peace Prayer has spread globally to inspire the pursuit of peace. It's been translated into dozens of languages, set to music by composers worldwide, and quoted by well-known leaders, cementing its influence across cultures and generations. Though widely attributed to St. Francis of Assisi, the true author of the prayer remains unknown. According to Kevin Flannigan, "The first appearance of the prayer occurred in France in 1912 in a small magazine called *La Clochette* (*The Little Bell*), published in Paris by a Catholic association known as La Ligue de la Sainte-Messe, "The Holy Mass League," founded by a French priest, Father Esther Bouquerel (1855–1923)."[6] Published without any attribution to an author, it was titled, "A Beautiful Prayer to Say During Mass."

In general, the Peace Prayer can be understood as follows:

- *Section 1: What.* The petitioner understands that instruments of peace provide antidotes to help alleviate internal and external human conflict.
- *Section 2: How.* The petitioner recognizes that instruments of peace surrender self-centered interests and desires to serve the greater good.
- *Section 3: Why.* The petitioner believes that instruments of peace find fulfillment paradoxically through selflessness and sacrifice.

While the petitioner asks God to be made an instrument of peace, the prayer offers no specific instructions for how that happens. That's what the rest of this book is meant to offer by way of inspiration, encouragement, and practical guidance.

Having grown up with this prayer and now revisiting it decades later, I see it not only as an inspiring hope but also as a meaningful road map for Christian living. Before we explore the directives found in the Peace Prayer, however, we should first examine its theological foundations.

UNDERSTAND THE THEOLOGY

For readers familiar with the Bible, the Peace Prayer appears to be shaped by Isaiah 61 and echoed in Luke 4, as in the following discussion. In particular, the juxtaposition of words within the prayer demonstrates both the mission and power of God to take what is wrong and make it right; what is broken and make it whole; what is absent and bring it to fulfillment. Understanding this framework is important for anyone seeking to become more like Jesus through the Peace Prayer.

Recognize the Anointed One

The prophet Isaiah lived, wrote, and spoke to leaders in Jerusalem and elsewhere throughout Judah in the eighth century BC. However, Isaiah 61 was likely composed during or just after the Babylonian exile (ca. 586–539 BC), well after he lived. For this reason, some scholars believe the book of Isaiah is a composite work written by multiple authors over time.[7] Amazingly, this Scripture looks ahead to the coming Messiah—as well as his servants (us)—who will demonstrate the good news of God's Kingdom. So the passage begins:

> The Spirit of the Sovereign Lord is on me,
> because the Lord has anointed me.
>
> ISAIAH 61:1

The Hebrew word rendered "anointed" is *mashach* (pronounced "mah-SHAK"), the root of the English word *messiah*.[8] Here, "me" refers to the Messiah—someone uniquely chosen and anointed by God. From the prophet's perspective, this Anointed One had not yet come. But looking back, Christians came to understand that Isaiah was prophesying about Jesus Christ. In fact, the title "Christ" comes from the Greek word *christos*, meaning "anointed one."

Isaiah goes on to describe the Messiah's mission:

> . . . to proclaim good news to the poor.
> He has sent me to bind up the brokenhearted,
> to proclaim freedom for the captives
> and release from darkness for the prisoners,
> to proclaim the year of the Lord's favor
> and the day of vengeance of our God,
> to comfort all who mourn,
> and provide for those who grieve in Zion—
> to bestow on them a crown of beauty
> instead of ashes,
> the oil of joy
> instead of mourning,

and a garment of praise
 instead of a spirit of despair.
They will be called oaks of righteousness,
 a planting of the Lord
 for the display of his splendor.

ISAIAH 61:1-3

While we can't be certain, the Peace Prayer does appear to be rooted in this passage. Notice the oppositional concepts:

- captivity vs. freedom
- darkness vs. release
- grief vs. comfort
- ashes vs. crowns of beauty
- sackcloth vs. garments of praise
- spirit of despair vs. display of God's splendor

Some 2,700 years later, it's easy for us to spiritualize these statements as referring only to a future in heaven. Yet the Anointed One brings good news to people on earth right now. Those lacking resources will be replenished. Hearts that have been broken by disappointment or betrayal will be healed. The fog of mental or emotional darkness will be lifted, and those who are guilty will find forgiveness and freedom.

As for his people, instead of dusting themselves with ashes to indicate a humility that comes from desolation or ruin, they will wear a crown or "stylish hat" and bathe in the oil of joy. Instead of wearing sackcloth, an outward sign of mourning, repentance, or abasement, they will be clothed in garments of praise. Instead of bending low in a spirit of despair, they will stand tall in the righteousness of God as a visible testimony to his glory.

In short, the Anointed One gives us what we don't deserve (i.e., grace) and withholds from us what we do deserve in terms of judgment and punishment (i.e., mercy). The Christ avenges wrongs perpetrated upon those who trust him, comforts those who mourn loss, and restores the hope of those who grieve.

Embrace the Anointed One

Fast-forward to the events of Luke 4, which occurred at the beginning of Jesus' public ministry, around AD 27–30.

Following his temptations in the Judean wilderness, Jesus journeyed north to Galilee "in the power of the Spirit, and news about him spread throughout the whole countryside" (Luke 4:14).[9] Jesus was very familiar with Galilee, having been raised in one of its towns.[10]

According to Matthew, it was during this time that news about Jesus spread throughout Galilee because he had been "teaching in their synagogues, proclaiming the good news of the kingdom, and healing every disease and sickness among the people" (Matthew 4:23).

Soon Jesus came to "Nazareth, where he had been brought up, and on the Sabbath day he went into the synagogue, as was his custom" (Luke 4:16). Keep in mind this was "his" synagogue, which he likely attended with his parents, Joseph and Mary. In other words, Jesus was well known in Nazareth and its synagogue. For this reason, it's not surprising that they yielded to Jesus as he stood to read, when "the scroll of the prophet Isaiah was handed to him" (Luke 4:16-17). Luke continues:

> Unrolling it, [Jesus] found the place [in Isaiah 61] where it is written:
>
> "The Spirit of the Lord is on me,
> because he has anointed me
> to proclaim good news to the poor.
> He has sent me to proclaim freedom for the prisoners
> and recovery of sight for the blind,
> to set the oppressed free,
> to proclaim the year of the Lord's favor."
>
> Then he rolled up the scroll, gave it back to the attendant [of the scrolls] and sat down. The eyes of everyone in the synagogue were fastened on him. He began by saying to them, "Today this scripture is fulfilled in your hearing."
>
> LUKE 4:17-21[11]

This is the culmination of Luke's argument.[12]

In other words, Jesus didn't just stumble upon this passage. Rather, he chose it intentionally—as a pronouncement. Without question, Jesus understood himself to be the Anointed One of Isaiah 61, the promised Messiah sent by God "to proclaim good news . . . the year of the Lord's favor." Courageously, he embraced his identity in public and made clear to all present that he had been sent to usher in a new chapter in the history of God's people—an age in which love, grace, and mercy would bring both closure and fulfillment to an era marked by law, condemnation, and judgment.

By self-identifying in Luke 4 as the Christ of Isaiah 61, Jesus also identified himself as the fulfillment of another messianic prophecy previously recorded elsewhere in Isaiah. This, too, would have been apparent to those who heard Jesus speak in the synagogue that day and were familiar with this prophetic passage:

> "For a Child will be born to us, a Son will be given to us;
> and the government will rest on His shoulders;
> and his name will be called Wonderful Counselor, Mighty
> God,
> Eternal Father, Prince of Peace."
>
> ISAIAH 9:6, NASB

Beyond its reference to the coming Messiah as God Incarnate, the title "Prince of Peace" is a translation of the Hebrew *sar shalom*, which some have rendered "the one who removes all peace-disturbing factors and secures the peace."[13] In hindsight, it is through his suffering, death, and resurrection that Jesus (the Christ) makes possible peace with God and with one another, far beyond what we might expect or feel in any given moment. He also offers peace to those struggling to find it in the midst of earthly worries, doubts, and fears. Simply put, Jesus alone is able to remove every "peace-disturbing factor," securing peace for us in this life and the life to come.

Walk in His Anointing

Jesus, the Anointed One, rescues and redeems all who receive his gifts of grace and mercy. But these gifts aren't just for us—they're meant to be shared. That's why Christ expects those redeemed to walk in his anointing—to live empowered by his Spirit and aligned with his purposes. As Isaiah writes:

They will rebuild the ancient ruins
  and restore the places long devastated;
they will renew the ruined cities
  that have been devastated for generations. . . .
And you will be called priests of the Lord,
  you will be named ministers of our God.

ISAIAH 61:4, 6

When we walk in the benefits of Christ's anointing, we become the "Spirit-empowered servants" of grace and mercy described in Isaiah 61. Through us, "the Lord God will cause righteousness and praise to spring up before all the nations" (Isaiah 61:11, NASB). As we continue in his anointing, we grow more like Jesus—true instruments of peace.

IDENTIFY WITH CHRIST

Identifying with Christ means not only believing that Jesus is God but also embodying his anointing. In doing so, we become instruments through whom Christ can remove the disturbing factors keeping those we know and love from experiencing spiritual, mental, or emotional peace—with God, within themselves, and with others.

It's no secret: Americans today are divided along lines of color, class, and culture as well as religion and politics. Christians, too, are often at odds with one another over these very same issues. Through intentional effort and by becoming instruments of peace, we can make a difference in the lives of others. While we may not be able to broker peace between nations, we can bring peace to those within our reach who are similarly troubled by internal pain, fear of the future, or relational conflict.

Even so, we should acknowledge that peacemaking is not easy. Realizing measurable impact will require a purposeful, sustained effort of prayer, patience, and persistence over time. More than that, we should expect to be misunderstood, misjudged, or maligned along the way, especially by those who benefit from division. In such moments, we should remember that even the Prince of Peace endured the same. As we follow in his footsteps, why should we expect anything less?[14]

In light of this biblical insight from Isaiah 61 and Luke 4, we're now ready to explore the specific directives of the Peace Prayer. Let's begin by asking: What does it take to defuse hate with love?

QUESTIONS FOR REFLECTION

1. Take a moment to slowly read the Peace Prayer. How might you memorize it? As a challenge to yourself, set a date by which you will try to have it memorized.
2. How should understanding Christ's anointing inform your daily walk with Jesus? What role and responsibilities should you assume as one who identifies with him?
3. Has there ever been a time in which you were unexpectedly drawn into a divisive debate or otherwise sparked a disagreement among those you know? How was the tension resolved? What was required of you or others involved to settle the matter amicably?

PART 2

Empowered by Christ

CHAPTER 3

Spread Love

Where there is hatred, let me sow love.

In the spring of 1994, while I was serving as a student ministries pastor in Little Rock, Arkansas, our team launched an eight-week series for tenth- through twelfth-grade students called *Point-Counterpoint*. It was designed to help teens think deeply about particular topics of public and biblical interest. To that end, we enlisted local leaders with divergent opinions to speak each week.

One night students heard from a Messianic Jew, and the following week from a local rabbi representing Reformed Judaism.[1] On another occasion, the conservative founder of a political organization spoke in support of traditional family values, followed seven days later by the leader of a local women's group advocating for the LGBT community. Even Mike Huckabee, Arkansas's lieutenant governor at the time and a staunch Republican, came to champion his pro-life position. To share a pro-choice perspective, I invited a Democrat recently appointed as the executive director of a nationally recognized progressive organization.[2] I'll refer to her as Michelle.

Prior to the series, we prepared our students to listen well and show each speaker respect, regardless of their own thoughts or opinions on any particular topic. In addition, students gave standing ovations each week following the presentations, while we presented each speaker with a small plaque in appreciation.

So on the night that Michelle spoke while I was handing her a plaque, as the students stood clapping in a demonstration of respect, she leaned over and whispered in my ear. Surprised that a theologically conservative Christian youth group would do so and with sincere gratitude, she said, "My first standing ovation!"

In the years that followed, I occasionally reached out to Michelle. For instance, I invited her to be my guest on a local Christian talk radio program that I hosted called *Conversations*. In reply, she said, "Mark, if you weren't involved, I wouldn't accept." Prior to planting Mosaic, I asked Michelle to join me for lunch. It was the spring of 2001, and I wanted to share my vision to plant a multiethnic and economically diverse church in the heart of Little Rock's urban center. Specifically, I wanted her opinion: Was there truly a need for such a church? Was this the right time to start one? And if so, did she believe I was the one to lead it?

Michelle shared with me over lunch that she held a Bachelor of Arts degree in the Special Honors Curriculum at Hunter College, City University of New York, with an emphasis in Religious Studies. I also learned that she had studied Philosophy of Religion as a graduate student at Columbia University. *Who would have thought?* I wondered in the moment, knowing she was not a Christian. As we left the restaurant that day, Michelle turned and said, "Mark, you're the only pastor that's ever reached out to me relationally or asked my opinion about anything. Thank you, it means a lot."

Over the years, I've become even more aware of the need to lay aside preconceived notions—of who's right or wrong, good or bad, friend or foe—in order to represent Jesus well. Especially today, Christians must intentionally extend love and disavow hate at every turn if we are to have any influence or impact on open skeptics, wounded cynics, and lukewarm believers.

Since losing touch with Michelle, I've often wondered: Did a show of respect one night from a Christian youth group do more than elicit a feeling of gratitude? Did our interactions ever move her from philosophical fascination with religion to an encounter with the God of unconditional love?

Likely, I'll never know.

Still, I do know that Michelle—and others like her—may never choose to follow Jesus unless Christ-centered peacemakers show up with radical love in a world overcome by hate.

PURSUE GROWTH

In 1960, six-year-old Ruby Bridges became the first Black student to attend the otherwise all-white William Frantz Elementary School in New Orleans. Each day, she faced hostile crowds hurling insults and threats in her direction as she walked to school. Despite this, Ruby prayed for her persecutors and asked God to forgive them. Her remarkable story of faith and forgiveness was later documented in a children's book by psychiatrist Robert Coles.[3]

Ruby's story reminds us that even in the face of real threats and fear, we can help break the cycle of hatred by determining to be different. If we are to be instruments of peace, we'll need to lay aside our justifications for anger and represent Jesus well, no matter how difficult it is or feels in the moment.

Sadly, unrestrained expressions of outrage, animosity, and hatred permeate every corner of public and private life today. Sometimes this anger is directed at the church and its leaders, but Christians also contribute to the problem. Hateful words are too often spoken by believers toward those with differing political, cultural, or theological views. Such behavior makes it challenging to follow the apostle Peter's instruction: "Do not repay evil with evil or insult with insult" (1 Peter 3:9).

Make no mistake: Threats and fears, whether real or perceived, are at the root of hateful exchanges and rhetoric that divide individuals or demographic groups. While we may feel justified in moments of outburst, we know deep down that this is not the way of Jesus. We should instead determine to be different—and we must if we are to become more like him.

True ambassadors of Christ-centered peace are guided by faith and governed by love. They guard their hearts, minds, and tongues in order to resist the natural temptation to hate those who threaten us or whom we fear for any reason. We should recognize that fear hinders Christlike love. As peacemakers, we cannot let it keep us from faithfully walking in his anointing.

RESPOND IN FAITH

In a letter written to early Christians facing hardship, Peter encouraged believers to be steadfast in doing good. He asked, "Who is going to harm you if you are eager to do good? But even if you should suffer for what is right, you are blessed." So Peter exhorted his readers, "Do not fear their threats; do not be frightened" (1 Peter 3:13-14).

These words paraphrase the prophet Isaiah. Some seven centuries before Peter penned his first epistle and 2,700 years before our own time, Isaiah wrote,

> Do not call conspiracy
> everything this people calls a conspiracy;
> do not fear what they fear,
> and do not dread it.
> The LORD Almighty is the one you are to regard as holy,
> he is the one you are to fear,
> he is the one you are to dread.
>
> ISAIAH 8:12-13

The Hebrew word translated as "conspiracy" is *qesher* (pronounced "KEH-sher"), which refers to an "(unlawful) alliance."[4] The related verb *qashar* (pronounced "kah-SHAR") means "to bind, tie, league together, conspire."[5] As for fear of the Lord, the Hebrew suggests that he alone should be the focus of our reverence—so much so that we are terrified of being aligned with other beliefs, practices, or philosophies of this world. To regard the Lord as holy is to recognize that he is wholly other—set apart.

To be sure, threats and conspiracies of various kinds have always been part of the human experience, and always will be. Many of these continue to directly challenge Judeo-Christian faith and practice. In the face of uncertainty, fear often drives human reaction, while faith compels a godly response. Accordingly, instruments of peace counter hate by embodying love.

My colleague of nearly twenty-five years, Harry Li, once spoke to the personal and emotional challenges many of us face in extending love when opposing points of view, personalities, preferences, and beliefs are in play.[6] In a sermon referencing Paul, Harry explained that Jesus offers the clearest example of how to love those who hate us—or whom we might otherwise see as enemies. Quoting Paul, Harry said:

> God demonstrates his own love for us in this: While we were still sinners, Christ died for us. . . .
>
> For if, while we were God's enemies, we were reconciled to him through the death of his Son, how much more, having been reconciled, shall we be saved through his life!
>
> ROMANS 5:8, 10

The Greek word *echthros* (pronounced "ek-THROS" and translated here as "enemies") can mean "hateful," either as something offensive or active hostility.[7] Paul explains that in our sinfulness—before being reconciled to God through Christ's death on the cross—we were hostile toward God. However, Jesus did "not repay evil with evil or insult with insult" (1 Peter 3:9). Rather, he responded to hate in a way that revealed the power of unconditional love, led us to repentance, and opened the way for our salvation.

While facing threats, fear, and hate, we should remain poised in purpose, anchored in faith, and respond with love, looking to Jesus as our example.

CREATE SPACE

To love others as Christ loves us requires self-discipline—a willingness to sacrifice wants, needs, and rights for the greater good of fulfilling God's purpose in the life of another.

Later in 1 Peter, the apostle exhorts us to "love each other deeply, because love covers over a multitude of sins" (4:8). This suggests that the way to reach nonbelievers is not through words and acts of judgment, condemnation, or cancellation, which only serve to push people away from Christ, Christians, and the church. Rather, the way to reach them is through empathetic acts that reflect Jesus' unconditional love—a love that invites, but does not demand, self-examination; a love that creates space for the Holy Spirit to move hearts in his way and time, so that others might repent and believe.

Again, Jesus is our example:

- He refused to go along with the seemingly justified condemnation and vitriolic attack by "teachers of the law and . . . Pharisees" against a woman caught in adultery (John 8:1-11).
- He refused to stand with "all the people" in their hatred of Zacchaeus, a chief tax collector whose wealth had accumulated through unjust profiteering (Luke 19:1-10).
- He refused to avoid a Samaritan woman at Jacob's well, choosing instead to lovingly share the truth with her (John 4:1-42).

In every instance, Jesus refused to condemn or "cancel" individuals twisted by sin's hatefulness, those regarded as enemies of God. He did not view these individuals for who they were at the time—guilty on all counts. Rather, he saw the adulterous woman, Zacchaeus, and the Samaritan through eyes of grace and mercy; as forgiven; and for who they could become. Each one, in turn, responded accordingly, compelled by love.

LOVE UNCONDITIONALLY

No verse in the Old Testament says, "Hate your enemies." Jesus corrected the erroneous interpretive commentary of religious leaders that informed Jewish people in the first century.[8] According to Matthew, Jesus said:

> "You have heard that it was said [by interpreters of the law], 'Love your neighbor and hate your enemy.' But I tell you, love your enemies and pray for those who persecute you, that you may be children of your Father in heaven."
> MATTHEW 5:43-45

When Jesus said, "love your enemies," he used the Greek word *agapate* (pronounced "ah-gah-PAH-the"), an imperative form of the word *agapaō* (pronounced "ah-gah-PAH-oh"). In this context, the term likely means "to have a preference for, wish well to, regard the welfare of."[9] This isn't about sentiment—it's a conscious choice to act in good faith and extend grace, even to those who may oppose us. It is the kind of love God shows to humanity: self-giving, unearned, and unconditional. He calls us to love our enemies as God loves us: completely and unconditionally. This ties directly to his command "Be perfect, therefore, as your heavenly Father is perfect" (Matthew 5:48). When we love like this and pray for the people who hurt us, we reflect God's heart and provide a tangible witness of what it means to live as his children.

As I've suggested, it's a natural, instinctive reaction to hate those we fear or don't know personally—those whose beliefs or practices we find offensive. We're often quick to judge, condemn, or cancel those with whom we disagree. Rather than love people as Jesus does, many Christians today are isolating themselves—choosing to "shelter in place" or live in echo chambers that reinforce only what they already believe.

But Jesus expects more of us. He calls us to "go into all the world" and represent him well. We are not meant to remain bound by our natural human inclinations but to rise above them, walking in the supernatural anointing of Christ.

To help navigate these tensions, Christians have long leaned on the phrase "love the sinner, hate the sin." Yet this well-meaning sentiment often oversimplifies a far more nuanced challenge.

It's not that we are to "love the sinner" as if this means ignoring or condoning beliefs and practices that conflict with biblical truth. Even so, it is not our right or responsibility to scorn and vilify those with whom we disagree. James says it this way: "There is only one Lawgiver and Judge, the one who is able to save and destroy. But you—who are you to judge your neighbor?" (James 4:12).

We can spread love in a world filled with hate through consistent effort, practice, and reflection. Hard as it is sometimes, the Prince of Peace must remain our example. He cried out on the cross, "Father, forgive them, for they do not know what they are doing" (Luke 23:34). Like Jesus, we should live and act in ways that help anyone caught in sin to encounter God's unconditional love. By showing kindness and patience in difficult moments, we reveal Christ's love for all people—not only those who are easy to love. God sees every such effort and will honor it, shaping us into instruments of peace in a world desperate for love.

QUESTIONS FOR REFLECTION

1. Are there people, groups, or perspectives today that challenge your beliefs and values? Who or what are they, and how specifically do they create tension within you?
2. Do you tend to see people with whom you vehemently disagree as "enemies"? Are any of them otherwise your friends? How do you distinguish between your friends and others whose opinions you more naturally dislike?
3. How does Jesus' example challenge your thinking about hate and love? How might his interactions with others help you respond differently to perspectives other than your own?

CHAPTER 4

Extend Forgiveness

Where there is injury, pardon.

From our earliest days of playing with classmates in the schoolyard to interacting with adults later in life, each of us knows the sting of being personally called out, humiliated, or offended. Yet we often choose to forget, ignore, or excuse the times we've treated others similarly.

Nevertheless, the harm of unjust, unnecessary, or unprovoked offense can last for years. Some never get over the hurt and hold grudges for the rest of their lives. The pain becomes part of an internal narrative—a moment replayed in the mind like a looped recording etched onto the soul. If unaddressed, the hurt affects how we see ourselves and interact with the world. It erodes trust and impedes relationships. When lingering pain is triggered, it informs angry reactions and perpetuates resentment. This is how bitterness develops. This is how the soul is damaged.

Painful history cannot be erased, but it can be overwritten by the power and presence of Jesus in our lives. To be healed from offense, we'll need to forgive.

"PUT" PARDON

Most English translations of the Peace Prayer translate the original French phrase, *Là où il y a l'offense, que je mette le pardon* as "Where there is injury, pardon." However, a more literal translation is: "Where there is offense, that I may put pardon." This phrasing highlights the intentionality involved: A deliberate willingness to extend pardon or forgiveness is central to peacemaking. We must learn to dress the wounds of personal offense with the salve of forgiveness if we are to become instruments of peace.

By way of comparison, the word *pardon* implies that one cancels "a penalty due for an admitted or established offense," as in a criminal who receives a pardon, is released from prison, and has his or her record expunged.[1] On the other hand, the word *forgive* implies that one "gives up all claim to requital."[2] While both words convey relational impact, they are not synonymous. Since the Peace Prayer also addresses the idea of pardon again near its end, we'll explore the concept more specifically in chapter 13.

Perhaps having been hurt by the offenses of others, Peter asked Jesus, "Lord, how many times must I forgive my brother or sister who sins against me? As many as seven times?" Famously, Jesus replied, "Seventy times seven" (Matthew 18:21-22, CSB). Rather than reinforce Peter's internal narrative of resentment, Christ invited him to consider how often he himself would want to be forgiven. In doing so, Jesus led Peter to forgive.

Jesus went on to share about a king who once forgave the significant debt of a servant. By law, he could have sold the man's family into slavery to recover the funds. However, the king responded favorably to his servant's plea for more time to pay by canceling the debt and letting him go. Though having been shown mercy by the king, the same man later lost patience with a fellow servant who owed him much less. After demanding that the other man pay his debt, despite how his own pleas had resulted in being forgiven, he choked his fellow servant and demanded he repay what was owed. Meanwhile, he "had the man thrown into prison until he could pay the debt. When the other servants saw what had happened, they were outraged and went and told their master everything that had happened" (Matthew 18:23-31).

Jesus continued:

> "Then the master called the servant in. 'You wicked servant,' he said, 'I [pardoned] all that debt of yours because you begged me to. Shouldn't you have had mercy on your fellow servant just as I had on you?' In anger his master handed him over to the jailers to be tortured, until he should pay back all he owed.
>
> "This is how my heavenly Father will treat each of you unless you forgive your brother or sister from your heart."
>
> MATTHEW 18:32-35

The king's actions sound like those of a peacemaker—someone quick to extend forgiveness, grace, and mercy while remaining mindful of another's humanity.[3] Clearly, this king is self-aware and grateful to have benefited throughout his life from being forgiven.

In contrast, the servant's actions mirror the behavior of many today who are quick to claim offense at the words, beliefs, or actions of others. In doing so, they press for cancellation.[4] Public expressions of outrage often elicit sympathetic support from friends and social media followers, frequently in the absence of conveniently withheld facts from the other side of the story. Emboldened by such affirmation, retaliation is validated, retribution is pursued, and restitution demanded. In this way, outrage has become the normative response to real, perceived, or even manufactured offense.

The fact is, we live in an age of entitlement and narcissism, as expressed in these common underlying attitudes:

- *Everything is about me and for me.*
- *You owe me everything, and I owe you nothing.*
- *If you're not like me or with me, you're against me.*

Such attitudes, however, are unbecoming of Christians since they do not reflect Jesus' character. They are not in line with who God is, how he acts, or how he loves those created in his image.

BE HUMBLE

Becoming an instrument of peace requires surrendering our own will to the will of the Father (Luke 22:42). It means directing even our conflicted emotions toward a singular, greater goal: representing Jesus well and pointing others to him.

As Christ followers, we have been called, expected, and anointed—not to seek power or privilege for pride's sake, but to glorify God in everything we say and do. To become more like him, peacemakers will need to embrace a posture of humility and a mindset shaped by grace. Hard as it may be at times, we'll need to discipline ourselves as Christ did on the cross. In the face of unjust offense, we must find the strength to echo his words: "Father, forgive them, for they do not know what they are doing" (Luke 23:34).

The Greek verb used here, *aphes* (pronounced "AH-fes"; a form of the word *aphiēmi*), is often translated "forgive." According to Ron Marrs, professor of youth and pastoral ministry at Western Seminary in Portland, Oregon, it is one of two Greek words used in the New Testament for forgiveness.[5]

Marrs explains that *aphiēmi* has the sense of "loose" (as in release) or "let go."[6] According to the *Liddell-Scott Greek–English Lexicon*, the word can mean to "send forth" or "discharge."[7] It's the same word used in 1 John 1:9 where the apostle writes: "If we confess our sins, he is faithful and just and will forgive [*aphiēmi*] us our sins and purify us from all unrighteousness."

Marrs continues, "When we forgive someone with the idea of *aphiēmi*, we let something go. We don't bring it up again. We don't let it take over our hearts. . . . [To be sure,] forgiving others can take time when something extremely hurtful has been experienced because of the sins of others. But understanding God's plan for forgiveness helps a believer in the process of forgiveness. Cancel the debt. Let it go."[8]

With this in mind, it's important to recognize that forgiveness—and the subsequent release of someone from offending words or actions, and restitution—does not depend on the offender. It is something entirely within our power. Likewise, forgiveness does not require reconciliation.

On the differences between forgiveness and reconciliation, Dr. Stanisław Głaz, a Jesuit priest and professor of philosophy at Ignatianum University in Krakow, Poland, writes,

> In human life, there are such phenomena as forgiveness and reconciliation. Both are connected with guilt and harm. They concern the wrongdoer and the harmed person, because forgiveness is a matter for the [harmed] person and is always possible, while reconciliation (with the wrongdoer) is not always possible, and depends on the attitude of the other person. . . . [Thus] forgiveness is an internal experience . . . the internal decision of the [harmed] individual.[9]

Simply put, we shouldn't wait for someone to ask our forgiveness. We can forgive from a distance whether or not there is ever an admission of guilt or apology received.

While forgiveness is always right, reconciliation is not always wise. In some cases, including those involving abuse or deep betrayal, it may not be safe or appropriate. Still, for our own emotional, spiritual, and physical well-being, we can and should release others from the debt of their offense. Otherwise, we remain chained to the offender, held hostage to the harm they caused.

FORGIVE YOURSELF

Earlier, I mentioned my high school's motto was "Men for Others." At the top of every test or paper we turned in, we were expected to write "AMDG." These initials abbreviate the Latin phrase *Ad Majorem Dei Gloriam*, meaning, "For the Greater Glory of God."[10] To this day, it inspires my life and work—not that I always live up to the ideal. Even so, AMDG remains a "north star" that guides my sense of identity, calling, and purpose.

That said, let me be honest. I've now served more than forty years in full-time ministry, but most days, I feel more sinful than saintly—like Paul, who writes:

> It is a trustworthy statement, deserving full acceptance, that Christ Jesus came into the world to save sinners, among whom I am foremost. Yet for this reason I found mercy, so that in me as the foremost [yet pardoned] sinner, Jesus Christ might demonstrate [to others] His perfect patience as [I become for them] an example [of his divine mercy] for those who [might someday through their interaction with me] believe in Him for eternal life.
> **1 TIMOTHY 1:15-16, NASB**

When it comes to forgiveness, it's not so much the offenses of others that trouble me as much as my own. The hardest person to forgive is often myself—especially when I offend God or someone else. In times of personal struggle or failure, I've found that appropriating God's forgiveness, grace, and mercy is far more difficult than extending those same gifts to others in their moments of weakness or confession.

We must be careful not to take God's grace for granted, as if forgiveness grants us license to sin. In fact, Paul also addresses this:

> What then? Shall we sin because we are not under the law but under grace? By no means!
> **ROMANS 6:15**

Nevertheless, given our inherent human weakness, we sometimes need to lean upon God's grace and mercy to sustain us through a moment or season of struggle until we can again walk the path of holiness in good conscience. As the late Billy Graham explained, "The closer you get to Christ, the more sinful you're going to feel."[11]

This deepening awareness of our sin can cause us to question our worthiness—not only to receive God's love but to be used by him as instruments of peace. In such moments, we may wonder if our failures disqualify us from serving his purposes. But even when we fall short or feel unworthy, our security in Christ remains firm. God's love for us never fails. In truth we were never qualified in the first place—only redeemed by Christ and made useful to him.

With this confidence, Paul writes:

> Can anything ever separate us from Christ's love? Does it mean he no longer loves us if we have trouble or calamity, or are persecuted, or hungry, or destitute, or in danger, or threatened with death [or if and when we fail him]? . . . No, despite all these things, overwhelming victory is ours through Christ, who loved us.
>
> And I am convinced that nothing can ever separate us from God's love.
>
> **ROMANS 8:35, 37-38, NLT**

Over the course of my adult life, while failing miserably at times "to walk in a manner worthy of the calling with which you have been called" (Ephesians 4:1, NASB), I've come to realize that my Sin (capital *S* intended) was not only once-for-all forgiven, but that Christ continues to "put pardon" toward me every day. Yes, I was once-for-all saved by grace through faith, at a moment in time years ago. But it's equally true that I am being saved daily by his grace while remaining loved by God the Father, secured by and kept for Jesus Christ.

BRING HEALING

Not long ago, I received a harsh text from someone. His words were sharp and cut deep, pointing to ways I had fallen short. He wasn't entirely wrong. Despite my best intentions, I'd made mistakes—said things I shouldn't have and done things I wished I hadn't. Guilt and shame hit hard, along with the painful realization that I couldn't go back and fix it.

At the same time, his accusations felt one-sided and unfair. Didn't he share some responsibility? My first instinct was to push back, defend myself, and fire off a response that highlighted his part in the breakdown.

However, I paused, took a breath, and chose a different path. I offered a genuine apology to take ownership of my part rather than defend or explain myself.

Later that evening, I received an apology from him as well. That moment of humility and forgiveness opened the door for reconciliation. It reminded me once again that holding on to offenses builds walls—but letting go makes room for peace.

Remembering that we are forgiven should compel us to forgive others. Having been justified by faith and now at peace with God (Romans 5:1), we should be all the more motivated to "be at peace with all people" (Romans 12:18, NASB). To do so, we'll need to resist the instincts of the flesh and respond with the mind of Christ when filled with anger or frustration toward another or tempted to condemn them. We can do so by withholding our words, checking our reactions, and expressing compassion in the face of offense.

We can do so by remembering, "There is only one Lawgiver and Judge, the one who is able to save and destroy. . . . Who [am I] to judge [my] neighbor?" (James 4:12).

As hostile as we've been toward him, it's only right to extend God's immeasurable grace and mercy to those who offend us. For as the Peace Prayer makes clear, in the measure that we forgive others, the forgiveness of others will be reciprocated.

As instruments of peace, let's learn to dress the wounds of personal offense with the salve of forgiveness and in so doing, become vessels of hope and healing.

QUESTIONS FOR REFLECTION

1. Think of a time you were challenged, criticized, or offended. What was your response? How long did it take to get beyond feelings of hurt or resentment, and why?
2. Who or what types of people in your life do you struggle to forgive? What holds you back from more quickly extending forgiveness?
3. Think about a time when you received forgiveness. How was it extended to you? How did being forgiven affect you?

CHAPTER 5

Inspire Faith

Where there is doubt, faith.

It was a difficult season. Called by God to leave his country, his people, and his father's household in obedience to God, Abram found himself in the Negev Desert together with his wife Sarai and their extended family, including his nephew Lot.[1] By this time, Abram had become rich in livestock, silver, and gold. Lot, too, had his own possessions, including large flocks of sheep, herds of cattle, and tents for his herdsmen.

According to the writer of Genesis, however, "The land could not support them while they stayed together, for their possessions were so great that they were not able to stay together. And quarreling arose between Abram's herders and Lot's" (Genesis 13:6-7).

In order to end the infighting and a potential for future conflict between them, Abram magnanimously gave his nephew a choice:

> "Is the entire land not before you? Please separate from me;
> if you choose the left, then I will go to the right; or if you

> choose the right, then I will go to the left." Lot raised his eyes and saw all the vicinity of the Jordan, that it was well watered everywhere—this was before the LORD destroyed Sodom and Gomorrah—like the garden of the LORD, like the land of Egypt going toward Zoar. So Lot chose for himself all the vicinity of the Jordan, and Lot journeyed eastward. So they separated from each other. Abram settled in the land of Canaan, while Lot settled in the cities of the vicinity of the Jordan, and moved his tents as far as Sodom.
>
> **GENESIS 13:9-12, NASB**

Wait a minute.

God had promised to bless Abram by giving him a land, a nation, and a name in return for his obedience (Genesis 12:1-3). Yet things took an unexpected turn when Lot departed. Since Lot chose the better part of the land, namely "the vicinity of the Jordan [valley] that . . . was well watered everywhere," with its warm climate and fruitful plains—Abram moved his family into the mountains "near the oaks of Mamre at Hebron" (Genesis 13:18, CSB).

Beyond the topographical change of plans, Abram was understandably concerned. The forced separation from his nephew came at a time when family meant everything—including personal security, financial stability, and long-term significance. A flood of doubt would have surely flooded Abram's mind in that moment. The journey so far had not been easy. Blessings and promises remained unfulfilled. Tribal disputes had occurred, and some family had already left him. Perhaps Abram felt foolish for having risked all that he had for nothing more than a promise of what might someday be.

It's not hard to imagine that following Lot's departure, Abram might have felt abandoned and discouraged. How would you feel when, after being promised a land "flowing with milk and honey" you end up in "a vast desert . . . [with] a range of hills rising to 900 metres [approximately 3,000 feet] above sea level" on which to somehow feed your cattle and survive with your family?[2]

Not surprisingly, it was right then that God intervened. I envision God drawing near to Abram in the moment, taking him on a walk, leading him to the top of a nearby mountain, and inspiring him to keep going. The narrative continues:

> The LORD said to Abram, after Lot had separated from him, "Now raise your eyes and look from the place where you are, northward and southward, and eastward and westward; for all the land which you see, I will give it to you and to your descendants forever."
>
> GENESIS 13:14-15, NASB

Isn't it interesting? When we lose hope, it often shows in our eyes, faces, and posture. That's why God told Abram to lift up his eyes—because his eyes were cast downward, his head hung low in discouragement. By asking Abram "How far can you see?" God invited Abram to look beyond his present circumstances toward the future with hope; to set aside lingering doubt and press on in faith.

CLING TO TRUTH

Doubt is a defining feature of today's culture, weaving its way into nearly every aspect of life. In a world saturated with conflicting information, many people wrestle with doubt—about truth, trust, and even God's sovereignty. Often, this uncertainty drives a need to control. When we doubt that God is truly in charge, we scramble to take matters into our own hands. We seek to impose our will or worldview—through political power, culture wars, or social media debates—instead of resting in his promises and plans.

The word *doubt* carries many shades of meaning. The *Merriam-Webster Dictionary* defines it as an "uncertainty of belief or opinion that often interferes with decision-making."[3] It questions truth claims, fosters distrust, and breeds suspicion or fear about what someone says or promises.

In contrast, *faith* is a "firm belief in something for which there is no proof; something that is believed especially with strong conviction."[4] The writer of Hebrews agrees: "Faith is the certainty of things hoped for, a proof of things not seen" (Hebrews 11:1, NASB). So the writer continues: "By faith Abraham, when he was called, obeyed by going to a place which he was to receive for an inheritance; and he left, not knowing where he was going. . . . For he was looking for the city which has foundations, whose architect and builder is God" (Hebrews 11:8, 10, NASB).

Like Abram, Christians are not immune to moments of doubt or disillusionment—seasons that shake our confidence in God and cloud decisions that would otherwise be made in faith. It's not so much that we doubt God's existence or his word as revealed in the Bible. More often, we wonder if God is truly paying attention; if he will respond favorably to our needs and concerns as it seems he does for others. While we may feel alone in such moments, God has promised, "[I] will not desert you or abandon you" (Deuteronomy 31:6, NASB). By clinging to this truth, we can find courage and strength to press on in faith through seasons of doubt, confusion, or frustration. Having done so, we can help others find peace as well.

EXERCISE FAITH

Faith is the foundation of true and lasting peace in our lives. The stronger our faith, the more secure we feel each day. When we choose to trust God's sovereignty, even in the midst of uncertainty, we let go of the need to control outcomes or harbor resentment. This trust fosters peace in our families, as faith gives us courage to forgive, humility to listen, and the grace to reconcile with others when needed.

For example, Dr. Lee Wilbur, an emergency room physician, and his wife Lori, a licensed physical therapist, cofounded Divine Mercy Health Center in 2018 to serve people who are falling between the cracks of public health care in central Arkansas. Driven by their Catholic faith, they established a 501(c)(3) medical mission rooted in compassion, dignity, and Christ-centered care. Each month the Wilburs bring medical professionals to a different parish in the region to serve the uninsured, underinsured, or underserved. More recently, they opened their first brick-and-mortar clinic on the campus of Mosaic Church in Little Rock, where they provide primary care, mental health, and social services at significantly subsidized rates to unhoused individuals and low-income families.

Together with others on their team, Lee and Lori stepped out in faith to launch the nonprofit initiative, bringing hope and healing to others in tangible ways. Rather than engage in culture wars or politicized rhetoric, their work quietly and tangibly makes a difference—one that inspires faith, cultivates hope, and reflects the Prince of Peace.

When we, or those we know, are consumed with doubt, faith is necessary to sustain us. Therefore, the unknown author of the

Peace Prayer asks for the grace to inspire faith in others, to help them press on through unfavorable times or circumstances.

Jesus said, "If you have faith the size of a mustard seed, you will say to this mountain 'Move from here to there,' and it will move; and nothing will be impossible for you" (Matthew 17:20, NASB). To be clear, it's not the quantity of our faith that accomplishes the impossible—as if we should feel guilt or shame for not doing enough when God's response fails to align with our desires. Rather, it's the qualitative object of our faith, Jesus himself, who can be trusted to remove obstacles in the way of what he calls us to become, pursue, and accomplish according to his will.

When doubts set in, consider Jesus, who passionately cried out in the garden of Gethsemane, "My Father! If it is possible, let this cup of suffering be taken away from me" (Matthew 26:39, NLT). Despite his fervent prayer—even considering who he was and all he had done—the Father did not respond in the way Jesus hoped. In other words, our Savior knows what it's like to have God say, "No, not now, not in this way. . . . Even still, trust me."

But asking God to take away his suffering was not all that Jesus prayed, nor did it prove to be the end of the story. He went on to pray, "Yet I want your will to be done, not mine." Thankfully, God replied to this prayer with a "Yes, okay!" Through Christ's atoning work on the cross and resurrection, we find strength to press on in faith through seasons of doubt.

In a moment of unimaginable physical, mental, and emotional suffering, and even the next day as he was dying on a cross, Jesus drew near to God by faith. God then drew near to Jesus and provided him with divine strength to endure an unfair, unjust, and untimely death. Similarly, when we help others maintain confidence in Christ, as hard as it might be for them, despair gives way to hope and doubt gives way to faith.

DON'T BE AFRAID

Digging deeper, we see that doubt is driven by fear that in turn fuels disillusionment and despair. Fear undermines trust, hope, and confidence. Unlike faith, fear leads us away from God. It discourages us from pursuing opportunities to discover our passions and fulfill Christ's purposes for our lives. Beyond that, fear keeps us from experiencing the joy that comes from chasing a dream.

To strengthen our faith and the faith of others, we should first identify the specific fear or fears fueling doubt, disillusionment, or despair. Toward this end, consider ten of the most common fears that give rise to doubt: the fears of

1. being wrong
2. making mistakes
3. personal or professional failure
4. the unknown
5. loss
6. rejection or abandonment
7. others' negative opinions
8. disappointing people
9. infirmity
10. death

Once a specific fear is named and acknowledged, it begins losing its grip on the mind, will, and emotions. In fact, not all aspects of fear are negative.

Author and poet C. JoyBell C. advises, "Don't be afraid of your fears. They're not there to scare you. They're there to let you know that something is worth it."[5] Likewise, Mark A. Riccobono, president of the National Federation of the Blind, observed: "The other side of fear—the positive power to stimulate action and unlock potential—is generally underestimated. If we resolve ourselves to face our fears, respect the power within those fears, and turn that power into action, we can take control of our own destiny, diminish the negative fears of others, and raise our expectations."[6]

This kind of understanding is part of what biblical authors allude to when they write, for example, "Fear God and keep his commandments" (Ecclesiastes 12:13), or "Serve the Lord with fear" (Psalm 2:11). By faith—and with a healthy understanding of fear, as Riccobono describes—we

- acknowledge and respect the Lord's power;
- yield to the Holy Spirit, allowing him to control our destiny and raise our hopes; and
- invite God to stimulate us to action and unlock our service in fulfillment of his purpose.

King Solomon explained, "The fear of the LORD is the beginning of wisdom" (Proverbs 9:10). Likewise, the prophet Jeremiah declared, "Blessed is the one who trusts in the LORD, whose confidence is in him" (Jeremiah 17:7).

With Solomon's words in mind, we should not fear or give in to doubt. Instead, we can let these moments deepen our faith, sharpen its focus, and strengthen its resolve—fixing our eyes on Immanuel, God with us . . . as did Jesus. When on the cross, at death's doorstep, he looked to his Father and prayed with confidence, "Into your hands I commit my spirit" (Luke 23:46).

REFUSE TO QUIT

In the spring of 2001, God was calling me to something different. For eighteen years, I had served local churches as a student ministries pastor. Now he placed on my heart—and on the heart of my wife, Linda—the dream of planting a church in Little Rock's urban center. We envisioned one where men and women of varying ethnic and economic backgrounds would will themselves to be one in the Lord for the sake of the gospel.

Very few people believed in the mission, and others thought we were crazy. Most doubted such a dream could be realized in Little Rock (of all places!).[7] More than that, some pointed out that I had never been a lead pastor or planted a church—something they considered a recipe for disaster. Others questioned my personality, temperament, and background as a westerner from Arizona now living in the South. One pastor said skeptically, "I've seen what Mark can do with resources. . . . It will be interesting to see what, if anything, he can do without them."

Thankfully, by God's grace, the dream became—and remains—a reality some twenty-five years later.

As I reflect on those early doubters, I remember my own doubts too. I recall my fear of being proven wrong, of making mistakes, and of failing. Like Abram, I strained for many years to see what God saw, while experiencing rejection and abandonment by those who once loved me well. Most of all, I feared disappointing Linda and our children.

Yet through all such doubt and fear, Linda and I held on to faith and to each other, though I can assure you, it hasn't always been easy. Even so, we've largely overcome the obstacles by trusting the One who brought us together and called us to plant a multiethnic church. In doing so, we have come to know the truth of Isaiah's words: "Those who hope in the Lord will renew their strength. They will soar on wings like eagles; they will run and not grow weary, they will walk and not be faint" (Isaiah 40:31).

Such stories are written only where passion, prayer, patience, and persistence abound. They are told only of those who let go of fear, hold fast to faith, and refuse to quit. They are the stories of those

> who through faith conquered kingdoms, administered justice, . . . who shut the mouths of lions, quenched the fury of the flames, and escaped the edge of the sword; whose weakness was turned to strength. . . . Women [who] received back their dead. . . . Others who were tortured, refusing to be released. . . . Some faced jeers and flogging, . . . chains and imprisonment. They were put to death by stoning; they were sawed in two; they were killed by the sword. They went about in sheepskins and goatskins, destitute, persecuted and mistreated. . . . They wandered in deserts and mountains, living in caves and in holes in the ground.
>
> These were all commended for their faith, yet none of them received what had been promised.
>
> HEBREWS 11:33-39

In spite of circumstances, all these—and countless others like them—pressed on in faith through seasons of doubt. One day their faith, and ours, will be fully rewarded, as will the faith of all who are determined to become more like Jesus.

QUESTIONS FOR REFLECTION

1. Can you recall when you felt like Abram—perhaps let down or abandoned by God? Even now, does disappointment linger? Imagine yourself in Abram's place. Hear God say to you, "Lift up your eyes." What do you see?
2. From the ten most common fears listed in this chapter that fuel doubt, which do you resonate with most? How have these affected your spiritual journey? What is needed to help overcome them?
3. Who in the Bible or history inspires you? In terms of representing Jesus well or as an instrument of peace, to what character traits are you drawn and how might you better weave them into your life?

CHAPTER 6

Cultivate Hope

Where there is despair, hope.

Long-distance open water swimming pioneer Florence Chadwick faced the dangers of despair. At thirty-four, she attempted to become the first woman to swim twenty-one miles across the Catalina Channel—from Catalina Island to Palos Verde on the California coast. But on July 4, 1952, the weather was uncooperative. The ocean was cold, the fog was thick, and the support boats were barely visible. Several times, sharks had to be driven away from her by gunfire.

As people across the country watched on television, Chadwick bravely kept swimming, her mother and coach riding nearby in a support boat, cheering her on. But after nearly sixteen hours in the water, and with less than half a mile to go, she finally gave in to the physical and mental exhaustion and asked to be pulled out of the water. Not long after, when she realized just how close she had been to completing the swim, she said, "I think if I could have seen the shore, I would have made it."[1]

Life often brings seasons of uncooperative weather: icy waters, heavy fog, and winds that obscure the way forward. In such times, we need Christ-centered "mothers and coaches"—those who draw near, offer support, and lift our spirits, just as Florence Chadwick needed during her historic swim. At other times, we must become that for others, reminding them that the shoreline is closer than they think and inspiring them to press on with hope through the struggle. In doing so, we become instruments of peace, empowered by the *sar shalom*, the Prince of Peace, who alone can calm the storm and remove peace-disturbing factors from our lives.

Someone once said, "People can live weeks without food, days without water, and minutes without oxygen, but not a moment without hope."[2] For this reason and others, the author of the Peace Prayer seeks God's help in bringing hope to those in despair.

TANGIBLY SUPPORT

Despair has become a pervasive challenge in our society, and mental health statistics in the United States paint a sobering picture. According to the National Institute of Mental Health, more than one in five adults—over fifty-nine million people—live with a mental health condition.[3] Rates of anxiety and depression have surged in recent years, particularly among younger generations.

The church is not immune to this reality. Studies show that nearly a quarter of practicing Christians have sought professional help for mental health concerns, while many others struggle in silence, uncertain where to turn. Despair can isolate, distort perspective, and erode a person's sense of purpose. Yet Jesus calls us to respond with hope, offering tangible support and the assurance that God is near though he may feel far away. For this reason, the author of the Peace Prayer asks for God's help in bringing hope to those in despair.

The truth is, there's hardly anything worse than feeling helpless to change a situation or losing confidence that you'll ever be happy again. Feeling powerless over your own future, or the lives of those you love, especially in matters of life and death, can be crushing. Even so, we are not alone. Jesus, who experienced and overcame death, understands despair and stands with us.

Still, if we're honest, we don't often sense his presence in the midst of despair. It can feel like he's a million miles away—and that's okay. Though we cry out, "Why, God?" or "Where are you?!," his love is deep and wide enough to hold our anger, absorb our questions, and steady our steps through valleys of shadow and death.

Cynics and skeptics may dismiss our faith in Jesus. But I've seen and personally experienced too many divine interventions—moments when only God could have known what I needed and came through in ways no one else could. At this point, it would take more faith for me to deny his existence than to believe in it.

Hope in Christ, then, is not a utopian fantasy: It's a fact anchored in biblical truth.

The word for "hope" in Greek is *elpis* (pronounced "el-PEECE"). The related verb, *elpō*, means "to anticipate, usually with pleasure." *Elpis* implies a confident expectation.[4] Where death is concerned, Paul writes:

> Brothers and sisters, we do not want you to be uninformed about those who sleep in death, so that you do not grieve like the rest of mankind, who have no hope. For we believe

> that Jesus died and rose again, and so we believe that God will bring with Jesus those who have fallen asleep in him. . . .
>
> After that, we who are still alive and are left will be caught up together with them in the clouds to meet the Lord in the air. And so we will be with the Lord forever. Therefore encourage one another with these words.
>
> 1 THESSALONIANS 4:13-14, 17-18

In this passage, Paul contrasts grief (or despair) in this life that accompanies death with hope of reunion in the life to come. Notice, however, he does not say despair is unexpected or that there is something wrong with Christians who grieve the earthly passing of those they love. Rather, Paul exhorts Christians not to give in to despair but instead to grieve with confident expectation in what is sure and certain; namely, that Jesus will come again to reunite believers in heaven. Especially in times of despair, Paul instructs us to encourage one another with expressions of hope.

Yet words of hope should not be dispensed in trite clichés. If so, they will hurt more than help.

STAY CONFIDENT

When our third child was delivered stillborn in 1995, Linda was forced to endure tormenting physical and emotional pain. Shortly after, a pastor entered the room and with a pat on the shoulder told her, "Don't worry, dear, you'll get over it. . . . Time will heal." Though well-intentioned, the pastor's words stung like salt in an open wound—sharp, unexpected, and unforgettable to this day.

In the months and years that followed, Linda and I processed our grief with hope anchored in faith. As we discovered, you never get over a child's death. Instead, you live with a heightened awareness of heaven's reality, and the confident expectation of one day being reunited with your child. In fact, Linda went on to "encourage one another with these words" through her groundbreaking book *Mommy, Please Don't Cry.* It begins by extending hope to parents grieving the loss of a child: "Mommy, please don't cry. . . . A beautiful angel carried me here."[5]

The apostle Paul also ties hope to faith when he writes, "Now may the God of hope fill you with all joy and peace in believing, so that you will abound in hope by the power of the Holy Spirit" (Romans 15:13, NASB). In times of despair, we can find hope through faith in the person and presence of Jesus. In fact, that's exactly where four men once sought and found help for a friend.

The Bible tells us that while Jesus was teaching in Capernaum,

> some men were carrying a man on a stretcher who was paralyzed; and they were trying to bring him in and to set him down in front of Him. But when they did not find any way to bring him in because of the crowd, they went up on the roof and let him down through the tiles. . . . And seeing their faith, He said, "Friend, your sins are forgiven you. . . . Get up, and pick up your stretcher, and go home." And immediately he got up before them, and picked up what he had been lying on, and went home glorifying God.
>
> **LUKE 5:18-20, 24-25,** NASB

That day, these men pursued hope by placing their faith in Jesus. The result? Their friend was healed.

DRAW STRENGTH

Not only can we find hope in in the person and presence of Jesus, but we can lean on that hope for comfort and strength in times of despair. This is what Job did in a season of great confusion, suffering, and sorrow. Having lost all his possessions, his children, and his health, Job did not lose faith in God. Rather, he said, "Though He slay me, I will hope in Him" (Job 13:15, NASB).

To be clear, there's nothing wrong with grieving a loss, being angry with God, or even questioning him in times of despair. Job does exactly that when he continues, "Nevertheless I will argue my ways before Him." Yet his aim is not to challenge God but to express his dependence on the One who remains sovereign in circumstances beyond his control. Job doesn't know how or when salvation will come—only who will bring it. In the meantime, he draws strength from God and finds relief.

We, too, can draw strength from hope in the midst of calamity. Centuries after Job, Isaiah wrote: "Those who hope in the LORD will renew their strength. They will soar on wings like eagles; they will run and not grow weary, they will walk and not be faint" (Isaiah 40:31). The Hebrew word translated in this passage as "hope" is *qavah* (pronounced "kah-VAH"). In some other Bible translations, it's rendered as "wait." *Qavah* connotes an eager, expectant waiting and not passive (delay).[6] It implies that something good is ahead, and that it will come from God.

Reflecting further on this passage, consider the outcomes for those who hope in the Lord:

- Those who need strength will find it renewed.
- Those who have fallen will once again rise.
- Those who are defeated will recall their purpose.
- Those on the verge of quitting will find a way to keep going, one step at a time.

As Isaiah declares, hope comes from placing our confidence in the Lord. But what about those who do not yet know him? That's where instruments of peace step in, becoming the hands and feet of Jesus, offering strength, comfort, and hope to those in despair.

CREATE OPPORTUNITIES

Peacemakers help others look to the future with expectant hope, just as Paul did. At a time in which his legitimacy was under fire, he wrote to the church in Corinth:

> We are hard pressed on every side, but not crushed; perplexed, but not in despair; persecuted, but not abandoned; struck down, but not destroyed. . . .
>
> Therefore, we do not lose heart. . . . For our light and momentary troubles are achieving for us an eternal glory that far outweighs them all. So we fix our eyes not on what is seen, but on what is unseen, since what is seen is temporary, but what is unseen is eternal.
>
> 2 CORINTHIANS 4:8-9, 16-18

Like Paul, we should look for opportunities to instill hope in others as they navigate their own moments of despair. While affliction is real, it is temporary. In time, "all things work together for the good of those who love God, who are called according to his purpose" (Romans 8:28, CSB). Confident of this, our hope in Christ can help those who do not yet know him

- find hope in the person and presence of Jesus,
- lean on hope for relief or remedy,
- draw strength from hope in the midst of calamity, and
- look to the future with expectant hope.

GENTLY GUIDE

When others find themselves lost in the fog of despair, our presence can be a lifeline. By drawing near, we remind them they are not alone, that peace is still possible, and that hope can be embraced—even in life's fiercest storms.

As we help guide others toward distant shores, we can gently point to promises that anchor the soul. These reminders of God's presence and truth offer steady hope when everything else feels uncertain:

- *His love never fails* (Lamentations 3:22). When others are in despair, let them know they are not forgotten or forsaken.

- *His purposes are still unfolding* (Jeremiah 29:11). When others are in despair, gently reassure them that this moment is not the end of the story.

- *His faithfulness hasn't changed* (Lamentations 3:23). When others are in despair, reflect stability and a steadfast commitment to Christ, especially when everything feels uncertain.

- *His truth steadies our perspective* (Deuteronomy 32:4). When others are in despair, help reframe panic with Christ-centered peace rooted in truth.
- *His promises remain unshaken* (Numbers 23:19). When others are in despair, hold hope for those too weary to embrace it themselves.
- *His ways are above our own* (Isaiah 55:8-9). When others are in despair, allow mystery to coexist with trust, since faith does not require full understanding.
- *His mercies begin fresh every day* (Lamentations 3:23). When others are in despair, lovingly remind them that tomorrow still holds new possibilities.

For Florence Chadwick, hope became her strength. Following her failed first attempt to swim across the Catalina Channel, Chadwick tried again on September 20, 1952, and despite heavy fog, this time she made it, later explaining: "As I swam I kept the shoreline in mind."[7]

Chadwick's determination to keep the shoreline in mind speaks to the power and promise of holding on to hope in times of despair. Her story reminds us that hope is not just a lifeline—it's a guiding light through life's most uncertain and challenging moments.

Peacemakers walk in Christ's anointing by cultivating hope in the lives of those who are struggling. They help remove peace-disturbing factors and restore hope. With this in mind, let's support and encourage others to keep swimming until the fog lifts and God's "plans to prosper you and not to harm you, plans to give you a hope and a future" (Jeremiah 29:11) are revealed. Yes, as Spirit-empowered servants of the Prince of Peace, let's come alongside those we know and love, echoing the words of the psalmist:

> We wait in hope for the LORD;
> he is our help and our shield.
> In him our hearts rejoice,
> for we trust in his holy name.
> May your unfailing love be with us, LORD,
> even as we put our hope in you.
>
> PSALM 33:20-22

QUESTIONS FOR REFLECTION

1. Have you ever felt an utter loss of hope or confidence, like you could do nothing to improve a difficult or worrying situation? Did anyone help you hold on to hope? If so, how?
2. Is there someone you know who is significantly discouraged or in despair? If so, what's caused their pain? Think of something tangible you can do to cultivate hope within them. When and how will you meet them at the bridge of Christ's humanity?
3. What is one new habit you could develop in order to cultivate hope in others? Likewise, what spiritual practices might you strengthen to remain hopeful in Christ?

CHAPTER 7

Shine Light

Where there is darkness, light.

In many ways, it feels like we're witnessing an unprecedented surge of pain, evil, and darkness in the world today. With rapid access to global news, graphic imagery, and a constant stream of crises in our pockets, it's easy to feel overwhelmed. While history has always been marked by immense suffering, what's different now is our instant and relentless exposure to pain through modern media.

But whether past or present, perhaps the deeper issue isn't the presence of darkness—it's the absence of Christ-centered light.

The late Brennan Manning (author of *The Ragamuffin Gospel*) once said, "The greatest single cause of atheism in the world today is Christians who acknowledge Jesus with their lips and walk out the door and deny him by their lifestyle. That is what an unbelieving world simply finds unbelievable."[1] If so, both the problem and the solution rest with Christians.

TAKE INITIATIVE

Darkness is an undeniable reality in this life, and Christians are not exempt from its reach. It surfaces in deeply personal struggles—the agonizing grief of losing a loved one, the heartbreak of divorce, or the suffocating grip of addiction. On a larger scale, darkness permeates not only local communities but entire nations plagued by poverty, injustice, and violence. In cities especially, where broken systems and deep inequities persist, questions of faith, purpose, and belonging often leave many searching for answers. These are the very moments when peacemakers are needed to step in, bringing clarity, comfort, and light to those navigating their darkest valleys.

There are two powerful accounts of beginnings in the Bible, each highlighting the profound significance of light overcoming darkness.

The first is found in Genesis, where the author describes the moment of creation:

> In the beginning God created the heavens and the earth. And the earth was formless and desolate emptiness, and darkness was over the surface of the deep, and the Spirit of God was hovering over surface of the waters. Then God said, "Let there be light"; and there was light. God saw that the light was good; and God separated the light from the darkness.
>
> GENESIS 1:1-4, NASB

To say that light was separated from darkness is to affirm that light drives out darkness—the two cannot coexist. Where light appears, darkness must retreat.

More than that, God declares light to be good. It brings life, joy, truth, and peace, while darkness represents death, pain, corruption, and ruin. When God says, "Let there be light," in the context of creation, it's as if he's also inviting us to do the same: to bring good light to others still walking in darkness.

The second profound biblical beginning is described by the apostle John, pointing beyond creation to eternity. Here again, light and darkness are central themes:

> In the beginning was the Word, and the Word was with God, and the Word was God. He was with God in the beginning. Through him all things were made; without him nothing was made that has been made. In him was life, and that life was the light of all mankind. The light shines in the darkness, and the darkness has not overcome it.
>
> JOHN 1:1-5

Notice that the Word to which John refers was not only present at creation but actively involved in it, having existed from eternity. A few sentences later, John clarifies who he has in mind: "The Word became flesh and made his dwelling among us. We have seen his glory, the glory of the one and only Son, who came from the Father, full of grace and truth" (John 1:14). As the rest of his Gospel confirms, John is speaking of Jesus.

It's important to recognize that the light of Christ's glory, grace, and truth was revealed only because Jesus made the first move. Unwilling that any should remain in darkness, he came down from heaven to enlighten us.

In his letter to the church at Rome, Paul recognizes that God reveals himself in a *general* sense through creation, writing, "His eternal power and divine nature—have been clearly seen, being understood from what has been made" (Romans 1:20). The psalmist echoes this truth:

> The heavens declare the glory of God,
> the skies proclaim the work of his hands.
> Day after day they pour forth speech,
> night after night they reveal knowledge.
>
> PSALM 19:1-2

Nevertheless, had Jesus not revealed himself to the world in a *special* way, humankind would have continued to grope in darkness, searching for the way, the truth, and the life (John 14:6).[2] In other words, darkness is not drawn to light; rather, light must enter darkness if the latter is to be dispelled.

So it is with peace—and with peacemakers. We are called to make the first move, drawing near to those experiencing confusion, pain, or fear, in order to reveal Christ's light and help dispel the darkness.

REFLECT THE LIGHT

In the Peace Prayer, the original French phrase *Là où il y a le doute, que je mette la foi* can be translated "Where there is darkness, let me put your light."[3] This appeal aligns with Christ's vision for the identity, purpose, and calling of those who follow him, as expressed in the Sermon on the Mount:

> You are the light of the world. A town built on a hill cannot be hidden. Neither do people light a lamp and put it under a bowl. Instead they put it on its stand, and it gives light to everyone in the house. In the same way, let your light shine before others, that they may see your good deeds and glorify your Father in heaven.
> MATTHEW 5:14-16

With this passage in mind, consider the following questions:

1. *Why are Christians the light of the world?* Immediately after being identified with Christ as peacemakers, Christians are also associated with him as those who bring light to the world.[4] Darkness persists wherever the light of Christ is absent—and believers are carriers of that light. Without the peace that frees the soul, people remain bound in moral and spiritual confusion.
2. *How are Christians to be the light of the world?* Just as Jesus declared, "I am the light of the world" (John 8:12), his followers are called to be conduits of light; not merely through words or beliefs but through tangible, transformative action. Everyone we encounter—"everyone in the house"—should experience the presence and benefit of Christ shining through us.
3. *What are Christians to do as the light of Christ?* Peacemakers shine light into personal, moral, and spiritual darkness by bringing clarity to confusion. In the midst of adversity, they help others see or find God, trust

> him, and cling to his steadfast love (Lamentations 3:22). These acts do not justify us before him; rather, we offer them in obedience—grateful for his love and forgiveness.

The light of Christ is not only displayed through the work of peacemaking but also reflected in how we walk according to his Word. Just as a mirror reflects only what's in front of it, so Christ's light shines brightly as the Word of God increasingly becomes for us "a lamp unto my feet and a light unto my path" (Psalm 119:105, KJV).[5]

CHECK YOURSELF

We are not the light itself. But like John the Baptist, we can serve as a compelling witness to it. Both Christians and non-Christians should be drawn to Jesus by the way we live and what we do. To that end, peacemakers practice self-control, ensuring that nothing we say or do distorts the reflection of Christ's light within us.

Self-control offers a necessary check for those inclined to speak out on the political, social, or judicial issues of our day. If we are to advance peace, we must balance our right to speak with the role to which we've been commissioned: namely, as ambassadors of Christ.

To be clear, speaking from conviction and serving as Christ's representative are not inherently at odds—but they are often confused or conflated.

For example, when Christians speak into politicized moments by affirming a specific party, policy, or politician, they risk criticism for not also addressing issues that reflect negatively on the same. Put simply, appealing only to the emotions or preferences of some can alienate others who disagree, preventing them from engaging with the very truth or perspective they may most need to hear.

This is not a call to silence nor a dismissal of potential Christian complicity, but a call to wisdom. As I've said before, there are many ways to speak . . . using words is just one of them.

Likewise, there are many ways to confront hypocrisy, injustice, and prejudice in the name of Christ. But if the way we speak serves only to close the ears or harden the hearts of those most in need of hearing our message, it may result in unintended consequences and diminished impact.

Whether through speech or other means, it is vital today for peacemakers to think, speak, and act with self-control and nuance. Yes, Jesus "spoke truth to power," but he did so with divine authority, perfect wisdom, and complete self-control. As fallible humans, we should proceed with great humility, recognizing our limitations before we presume to challenge others.

Jesus died with outstretched arms—both literally and symbolically—holding space for those on the right and on the left, so that all, not just some, might find hope and life in him. To become more like him, we must emulate that posture.

SERVE HUMBLY

In addition to practicing self-control, peacemakers must also embrace humility in order to be a light in the world.

Paul once wrote to the church at Philippi—a multiethnic congregation comprised of believing Jews and Gentiles, men and women, rich and poor. In Philippians 2, he describes humility as an attitude that empowers us to set aside personal preferences in order to rightly engage with and accommodate those who are, in some way, different from us.[6] To this end, he writes: "In your relationships with one another, have the same mindset as Christ Jesus: Who, being in very nature God, did not consider equality with God something to be used to his own advantage; rather, he made himself nothing by taking the very nature of a servant, . . . [and] humbled himself by becoming obedient to death—even death on a cross!" (Philippians 2:5-8).

While we're not called to die on a cross, peacemakers are called to die to self at times in order to reflect the light of Christ. Like our Lord and Savior, this means clothing ourselves in humility, putting the needs of others before our own.

According to Noah M. Wallace, "Comporting yourself with kindness, empathy, and understanding can foster positive relationships with others. By treating others with respect and dignity, you create an atmosphere of trust and mutual support. . . . For example, actively listening to others, offering help when needed, and resolving conflicts in a respectful manner can strengthen relationships and create a positive social environment."[7] This, too, describes the character, intentionality, and humility of a peacemaker.

PURSUE TRANSFORMATION

Photosynthesis is "the process by which plants use sunlight, water, and carbon dioxide to create oxygen and energy in the form of sugar."[8] Without light, this process could not occur. As sunlight is absorbed, water molecules are split and oxygen is released. "Photosynthesis literally replenishes the air we breathe."[9] Without photosynthesis, plants wouldn't thrive, and we wouldn't survive. In the same way, we cannot be spiritually transformed without the light of Christ. As Father Billy Swan from the Catholic diocese of Ferns in Ireland, writes, "When the grace of God comes to us from Christ in the Spirit (symbolized by sunlight), it . . . effects redemption by breaking down [sinful] elements in our nature (symbolized by carbon dioxide). The light of God's grace then transforms these harmful traits . . . into other elements that benefit us and others (symbolized by oxygen and sugar)."[10]

As Christians, we are not immune to the darkness that lingers in a broken world—nor are we spared from times of deep spiritual desolation that St. John of the Cross, a sixteenth-century Carmelite monk, described as "the dark night of the soul." In both poetry and prose, John spoke of this experience as a necessary, though painful, passage in the soul's journey toward deeper union with God.

Translator E. Allison Peers explains the dark night is "an inflowing of God into the soul, which purges it from its ignorances and imperfections, habitual, natural and spiritual. . . . Herein God secretly teaches the soul and instructs it in perfection of love, without its doing anything. . . . By purging and illumining it, He prepares [the soul] for the union of love with God."[11]

Reflecting on this concept, Dr. Karyn L. Wiseman writes: "But for Saint John of the Cross, the dark night was not about God being absent. . . . The poem was about the joy we find in the journey to unite with God. It is about the fact that God is present all the time but we go through a time of purging and illumination to find that union. We may not feel it, but God is there. Always."[12]

Dark nights of the soul can be triggered by many things—from fractured families and the sting of betrayal to job loss, financial instability, chronic illness, loneliness, or the exhaustion that comes from shouldering burdens without assistance or relief. While following Jesus doesn't make us immune to life's inevitable pain, he's promised to walk with us through it, offering strength and peace. Confident of this, we don't need to fear evil, wickedness, or adversity. As he promised, "I am the light of the world. Anyone who follows me will never walk in the darkness but will have the light of life" (John 8:12, CSB).

Grammy Award–winning singer-songwriter Sarah Jarosz captures the apparent contradiction of finding light through darkness in her song "Dark Road." At one point, she describes a journey down a long, empty road—a path marked by profound darkness that surprisingly leads to unexpected clarity. The final line of the song expresses this poetic paradox: the darkness gives way as the singer *falls up* into the light.

I love this curiously contradictory idea. So, too, may our encounters with others *fall up* into Jesus . . . ultimately, the One we must all find to know the truth and be set free.

QUESTIONS FOR REFLECTION

1. Reflect on a time of darkness in your life. Did anyone walk with you through it, shining a light into your life and providing comfort? If so, what did they do? How did it help aid your learning, recovery, or healing?

2. Have you regretted something you said when angry or hurt? How did you feel afterward? How can practicing verbal self-control help you reflect Christ's love?

3. Is someone in your life struggling with confusion, pain, or fear? What would it look like for you to shine the light of Jesus into a relationship, your community, or your workplace?

CHAPTER 8

Bring Joy

Where there is sadness, joy.

Linda and I have walked through many seasons of sorrow over nearly forty years of marriage. Both individually and together, we've endured deep emotional pain on nearly every front. Like so many others, we've faced personal, marital, parental, familial, relational, financial, and vocational hardships, in ways that were real, raw, and at times deeply regrettable. More than once, joy felt entirely out of reach.

While I'm not suggesting we're role models, time and time again we have rebounded by recognizing and responding to the same Voice that encouraged Abram to lift his eyes and look toward the future with hope—learning, like the psalmist, that "weeping may last for the night, but a shout of joy comes in the morning" (Psalm 30:5, NASB).

So we continue to play the long game—trusting that joy returns after sadness when we refuse to give up on ourselves or on God.

CONSIDER SADNESS

The *Cambridge English Dictionary* defines *sadness* as "the feeling of being unhappy, especially because something bad has happened" . . . "something that is not satisfactory or pleasant and makes you feel shocked or angry."[1] *Merriam-Webster* associates varying nuances as part of its definition of *sadness*, including

- "[being] affected with or expressive of grief or unhappiness: downcast";
- "causing or associated with grief or unhappiness: depressing";
- "of little worth"; and
- "of a dull somber color."[2]

It's no secret: Anyone who lives long enough will suffer hurt, rejection, loss, unfair treatment, and misunderstanding. These moments can bring deep sadness, making us question whether our hopes, dreams, or efforts were ever worth it. In times like these, we ask, *What's the point of going on?*

Unlike depression—which is a diagnosed longer-term mental health condition—sadness is generally temporary and situational. It's an emotion we move through, while depression often requires professional intervention and support.

Research affirms what many already feel: Emotional pain is all too common. The US Centers for Disease Control and Prevention (CDC), citing a 2023 National Health Interview Survey, found that 12.5 percent of adults over age eighteen reported regular feelings of worry, nervousness, or anxiety, and 5 percent of adults in the same age category reported experiencing depression.[3] While sadness is not the same as clinical depression, the overlap between them highlights just how pervasive emotional distress has become in our society.

Sadness can stem from a range of personal or communal sources. It may also manifest collectively, affecting entire communities in response to shared struggles such as injustice, violence, or economic hardship. The COVID-19 pandemic underscored this as millions faced isolation, financial uncertainty, and collective grief. It left many with a lingering sense of loss.

As I've observed, there are at least ten common causes of sadness:

1. *Sudden or unexpected shock.* When unanticipated moments shake us, sadness is a natural response.
2. *Circumstances beyond our control.* When things go wrong and we have no ability to change the outcome, we feel sad.
3. *Endings.* When seasons of life, relationships, or careers come to an end, sadness often rises. Likewise, when the last child leaves home to attend college, serve in the military, or get married, the transition stirs something deep within the soul.
4. *Regret.* When we dwell on past sins or personal failures, we can be overwhelmed by sadness.
5. *Limitations, flaws, or faults.* When we face the truth that we can't do it all, that our weaknesses are real, or that we've made mistakes, sadness will be present.

6. *Disappointment.* When things don't turn out the way we hoped or planned, sadness follows as we mourn what might have been.
7. *Physical health.* When we don't exercise or get enough sunlight, or when we overindulge in food and drink, both our bodies and our self-image suffer, and sadness takes root.
8. *Mental health.* When our minds are affected by substance abuse, mood swings, depression, loneliness, comparison, or covetousness, then debilitating sadness will be a constant companion.
9. *Unfulfilled yearnings.* When long-held dreams remain out of reach or do not come true, it makes us sad.
10. *The thought of inescapable death.* When terminal sickness is diagnosed, a parent dies, or we simply reflect on our own mortality, the shadow of death brings inevitable sadness.

Sadness is a natural part of being human, and there's nothing wrong with feeling it from time to time. In fact, emotions like sadness are part of what theologians describe as our *personhood*—the state of being an individual endowed with intellect (mind), emotion (feelings), and volition (will). As Dr. Philip Irving Mitchell notes, the biblical concept of the heart encompasses "the full person of a human being—the intellect, emotion, volition, even body."[4]

ANTICIPATE EMOTIONS

In the Bible, we see that God is personal . . . meaning he thinks, feels, and chooses. The psalmist describes God as experiencing sorrow: "Oh, how often they rebelled against him in the wilderness and grieved his heart in that dry wasteland" (Psalm 78:40, NLT). Similarly, Isaiah writes, "He was despised and rejected by mankind, a man of suffering, and familiar with pain" (Isaiah 53:3).

To deny God's emotions is to deny that he possesses personality. And because we are made in his image, we, too, experience the emotion of sadness.

In the Gospel of John, we're told that Jesus experienced sadness when he encountered Mary, just after the death of her brother Lazarus.

> When Mary came to the place where Jesus was, she saw Him and fell at His feet, saying to Him, "Lord, if You had been here, my brother would not have died." Therefore when Jesus saw her weeping, and the Jews who came with her also weeping, He was deeply moved in spirit and was troubled, and He said, "Where have you laid him?" They said to Him, "Lord, come and see." Jesus wept. So the Jews were saying, "See how He loved him!"
>
> JOHN 11:32-36, NASB

It was then that Jesus raised Lazarus from the dead, and sadness turned to joy.

CHOOSE JOY

Just as there's a difference between sadness and depression, there's also a difference between joy and happiness. According to David Brooks, opinion columnist for *The New York Times*,

> Happiness usually involves a victory for the self. Joy tends to involve the transcendence of self. Happiness comes from accomplishments. Joy comes when your heart is in another. Joy comes after years of changing diapers, driving to practice, worrying at night, dancing in the kitchen, playing in the yard and just sitting quietly together watching TV. Joy is the present that life gives you as you give away your gifts. The core point is that happiness is good, but joy is better. It's smart to enjoy happiness, but it's smarter still to put yourself in situations where you might experience joy.[5]

With these differences in mind, let's take a closer look at what joy is not:

- Joy is not derived from trite clichés.
- Joy is not dismissive of hurt or pain.
- Joy is not disconnected from reality.

We should also recognize that joy doesn't demand or expect that we will always be happy. Rather, in seasons of sadness, joy gives us a way to remain hopeful.

To be clear, joy is not necessarily tied to satisfaction with current circumstances or outcomes, but to our confidence in Christ. It flows from the surrender of ourselves by faith to his will.

Being joyful, then, does not mean that we are indifferent or immune to pain and problems. It means that even in hardship, we remain anchored in truth and guided by the Holy Spirit.

Now let's look at what joy *is*. Here's what the Bible says:

- *A strength that God gives.* "Do not grieve, for the joy of the LORD is your strength" (Nehemiah 8:10).
- *An expectation God fulfills.* "I cried to You for help, and You healed me. . . . Weeping may last for the night, but a shout of joy comes in the morning" (Psalm 30:2, 5, NASB).
- *An outcome of salvation.* "Restore to me the joy of Your salvation, and sustain me with a willing spirit" (Psalm 51:12, NASB).
- *A fruit of the Holy Spirit.* "The fruit of the Spirit is love, joy, peace, forbearance, kindness, goodness, faithfulness, gentleness and self-control" (Galatians 5:22-23).
- *A peace that guards our hearts and minds.* "Rejoice in the Lord always; again I will say, rejoice! . . . Do not be anxious about anything, but in everything by prayer and pleading with thanksgiving let your requests be made known to God. And the peace of God, which surpasses all comprehension, will guard your hearts and minds in Christ Jesus" (Philippians 4:4, 6-7, NASB).

From joy, we gain understanding (wisdom), discover significance (purpose), acquire security (confidence), and realize blessing (fulfillment). Ultimately, we choose joy by acknowledging life's complexity, affirming what is true, and trusting that God is with us in our sadness, even when it doesn't feel that way.

Joy is rooted in the belief that God remains in control. It's sustained by the conviction that he will one day restore us to wholeness. Such is the confidence that steadies our hearts and minds through seasons of sadness. It's a confidence we're called to help others find as well.

Joy is also anchored more in past experience and future hope than in present circumstances. With this in mind, we find joy as much through deliberate choices as through spontaneous emotion.

Finally, joy isn't passive—it must be cultivated as an active response to sadness.

According to Deuteronomy 16:16-17, God commanded Israel to gather in Jerusalem three times a year for weeklong festivals of remembrance, thanksgiving, and joyful celebration.[6]

- *The Feast of Unleavened Bread* was a spring gathering that commemorated Israel's flight from Egypt. The celebration served as a reminder of their liberation, faith, and journey from slavery to freedom.
- *The Festival of Weeks* was also held in the spring, and commemorated the giving of the Torah at Mount Sinai. This marked the covenant between God and Israel that established the moral and legal foundation for Jewish life.
- *The Festival of Tabernacles (Booths)* began five days after the Day of Atonement when the fall harvest was completed. It commemorated God's provisions and protection of Israel during their forty years in the wilderness.

At these festivals, the people of Israel recalled past experiences of both sorrow and joy. They reflected on God's character—the fact that he had always been with them despite how things may have appeared at the time—and on his purposes. They acknowledged God's steadfast love in the past and joyfully celebrated his continued sustenance of the nation. In response, the Israelites brought offerings to God just as he commanded: "No one should appear before the Lord empty-handed: Each of you must bring a gift in proportion to the way the LORD your God has blessed you" (Deuteronomy 16:16-17).

DEVELOP RHYTHMS

As peacemakers, we can help others rediscover joy by guiding them to remember and celebrate what God has already done. Like ancient Israel, we can also develop rhythms and practices that embed joy into our lives. In doing so, we cultivate an inner reservoir of joy that equips us to better navigate life's inevitable seasons of pain, confusion, and disappointment.

This kind of intentional, cumulative joy doesn't appear overnight—it builds slowly and steadily, much like compound interest.

Compound interest is a financial principle in which the interest earned on savings begins to earn interest itself over time. In other words, "With each passing year, your compounding interest grows exponentially until it exceeds your principal and is responsible for most of the growth in your account."[7] Similarly, joy compounds over time.

So how can we experience—and help others experience—this kind of joy? We can follow Israel's example:

- *Recall past experiences of joy and sorrow.* Regularly sit with the people in your life to review both the highs and lows. Remember: Some moments arise from our choices, some from the choices of others, and some are simply beyond explanation or control.
- *Reflect on God's character and presence in the past while praying to discover his purposes now.* Because God is eternal, he is not bound by time. Through Christ-centered meditation we can revisit past sorrows and discover he was there all along. Sit with Jesus, speak openly, and let him lead you from sorrow's darkness into the light of joy.
- *Recognize that Christ's steadfast love and sustaining provisions have always been, and will always be, yours.* God is as competent and in control today as ever. In private and corporate worship, praise him for who he is, thank him for what he has done, and trust that his purposes will become clear in time. Meanwhile, entrust your soul to a faithful Creator by doing what is right and good (1 Peter 4:19).
- *Respond by giving back to him something of yourself in return.* Generously use your time, skills, passions, and resources to bring joy to others—not to earn God's favor, but in gratitude for all he has done.

If you're a young adult, begin now to cultivate a joyful rhythm of recall, reflection, recognition, and response—one that will anchor your faith in the years ahead. If you're older, it's never too late to start. Like water released from a dam, joy can still flood your heart as you reflect on God's character, purposes, and steadfast love for you. More than that, as an instrument of peace, you can bring joy to others by encouraging them to do the same.

QUIET YOUR SOUL

In the third century, a man who was nearing death wrote the following words to a friend:

> It's a bad world, an incredibly bad world. But I have discovered in the midst of it a quiet and holy people who have learned a great secret. They have found a joy which is a thousand times better than any pleasure of our sinful life. They are despised and persecuted, but they care not. They are masters of their souls. They have overcome the world. These people are the Christians, and I am one of them.[8]

In times of great sadness, Christians may be down, but they're never out. Joy will come again to those who lift their eyes to the Lord—to those who remember whose they are, from where they've come, and in whose hands they remain. This kind of joy cannot be taken from them.

QUESTIONS FOR REFLECTION

1. Who or what consistently saddens or disappoints you? Think deeply about why and how it impacts you.

2. Reflect on how joy is more of a choice than an emotion. Does anything currently hinder your joy? If so, what? How might you recover joy not only for yourself but for others, too?
3. Could you experience joy in the midst of circumstances that remain unchanged? If so, how? What can you do to bring joy to others experiencing sadness?

PART 3

Engaged for Christ

CHAPTER 9

Seek to Comfort

Grant that I may not so much seek to be consoled as to console.

On August 28, 1988, three jets from the Italian aerobatics team Frecce Tricolori collided during an airshow at Ramstein Air Force Base in Germany. All three pilots were killed instantly, and the accident turned catastrophic when one of the jets crashed into the crowd. Seventy spectators lost their lives, and more than a thousand others were injured—making it one of the deadliest disasters in both aviation and airshow history.[1]

Arriving at Ramstein one year later to serve as junior and senior high school leaders for Catholic and Protestant youth on the base, as well as those from the nearby Kaiserslautern Army Depot (K-Town), Linda and I learned that many of the students had been at the airshow that day. One moment they were enjoying themselves; the next, they were running for their lives. Later, they helped first responders by handing out water, food, and blankets to the injured.

So imagine the compounding trauma when on August 29, 1990, almost two years to the day after the airshow disaster, a massive C-5 Galaxy transport plane crashed and caught fire just after takeoff from Ramstein. The plane was tasked to the Persian Gulf to deliver medical aid, food supplies, and aircraft maintenance equipment to American forces deployed in the region.[2]

Of the seventeen souls on board, only four survived; and among the dead was Capt. Bradley R. Schuldt, USAF.

Much more than a friend, Brad was a devoted follower of Christ with whom Linda and I shared a three-story house off-base in Ramstein Village. He was also a beloved volunteer in our youth ministry, who served students with passion, commitment, and joy.[3] According to his stepmother, Brad "had planned [following his time in the military] to be a clergyman and a commercial pilot."[4]

Setting aside our own grief, Linda and I spent the next several months consoling students and families in the aftermath of Brad's untimely, dreadful death. By so doing, we found consolation as well.

WELCOME THE PARADOX

My friend Harry Li identifies a subtle shift in the third part of the Peace Prayer from what is emphasized in the second part.[5] Whereas the second part centers on sowing seeds of peace into the lives of others, the third part introduces a counterintuitive yet profound spiritual truth: "Our deepest needs are often met not by seeking to have them met but by giving selflessly to meet the needs of others."[6]

Paraphrasing his words from a sermon on consoling others, Harry said:

> If you need love, show love, and in the process, love will come back to you. If you need to be forgiven, forgive others, and you will find forgiveness. Many times, when

we seek directly to have our needs met, we end up disappointed. In reality, it's not in the seeking but in the giving of ourselves to others that our own needs are met. This aligns with the paradoxical teachings of Christ: If you want to find your life, you must lose it. If you want to live, you have to die. If you want to be first, you must be last. If you want to be exalted, you must humble yourself.

All such teaching runs contrary to human wisdom and otherwise to how we are wired. This middle section of the prayer reminds us that when we meet the needs of others, our own needs will be met. In becoming an instrument of peace, we experience peace ourselves.[7]

DRAW NEAR

Grief, sadly, is intrinsic to the human experience. It has been so since Adam and Eve were banished from Eden—and later when they endured the unthinkable: the loss of one son at the hand of another.

In a world of more than eight billion people, grief is more visible and widespread than ever before:

- Natural disasters devastate entire regions, leaving survivors to grapple with loss and displacement.
- Mass shootings strike schools, workplaces, and houses of worship, cutting lives short and shattering our sense of safety.
- Wars ravage nations, displace millions, and leave behind trauma that echoes through generations.
- Domestic violence destroys families and dreams. The wounds do not fade with time—they linger in memories, scars, and patterns that ripple across generations.

Such pain is not confined to those who endure it directly. In our hyperconnected world, grief is amplified and widely shared, creating a collective sense of sorrow and uncertainty. With this in mind, the need for consolation has never been greater.

When we console one another, we affirm our shared humanity and common needs. A word of comfort, a compassionate presence, or a single act of kindness can become a lifeline for someone carrying the crushing weight of loss.

The word *console* means "to alleviate the grief, sense of loss, or trouble of" another.[8] Additional meaning can be found in a comment by English novelist and poet Ferdinand Mount, who wrote of Sir Kingsley Amis, "He was a tactful consoler and capable of great generosity to people in trouble."[9] Mount's insight about Amis aligns with Paul's understanding of God's great generosity toward us in times of trouble. Writing for a second time to the church at Corinth, Paul begins his letter:

> Praise be to the God and Father of our Lord Jesus Christ, the Father of compassion and the God of all comfort, who comforts us in all our troubles, so that we can comfort those in any trouble with the comfort we ourselves receive from God.
>
> 2 CORINTHIANS 1:3-4

Consolation, however, goes beyond simple acts of kindness. It's a divine expression of Christ's character, mirrored in those who seek to become more like him. When we weep with those who weep and carry one another's burdens, we participate in his healing work. As instruments of peace, followers of Jesus are uniquely called to step into the role of consoler, acting in obedience and love.

Many English Bibles translate the Greek word *paraklēsis* (pronounced "pah-RAH-klay-sis") as "comfort." Second Corinthians 1:3 might read "the Father of compassion and the God of all consolation, who consoles us in all our troubles." The difference in meaning is important to understand.

Paraklēsis is a noun related to the verb *parakaleō* (pronounced "pah-rah-kah-LEH-oh"). This word is made up of two words: *para* (pronounced "pah-RAH"), meaning "with" or "beside," and *kaleō* (pronounced "kah-LEH-oh"), meaning "to call." You might recognize it from when Jesus talks about the Holy Spirit, sometimes referred to as the Paraclete. In John 14, he says, "I will ask the Father, and he will give you another advocate [*paraklētos*, pronounced "pah-RAH-klay-toss"], to help you and be with you forever—the Spirit of truth" (John 14:16-17). Jesus also says, "If I don't [go away], the Advocate [*paraklētos*] won't come. If I do go away, then I will send him to you" (John 16:7, NLT).

With this in mind, the *paraklētos* (the Holy Spirit) is the one "called to come alongside" us. He is the one present in times of trouble, rendering help and strength. The term is often translated in English as "helper" or "comforter," but as such, Jesus' sending of the Holy Spirit to be at our side can be lost in translation.

Think about it: You can help or comfort someone by giving or sending something to them from a distance. But to truly console someone, you must be near and present, walking alongside them through a moment or season of need.

From this passage, we learn that God is the source of all consolation, that compassion is central to it, and that the Holy Spirit, sent by Jesus, is the One who draws near in times of trouble. In other words, consolation isn't merely about making someone feel comfortable. It's about embodying compassion through personal presence to help alleviate another's distress, grief, or fear.

GIVE ASSURANCE

We all feel overwhelmed at times by the crushing weight of life's troubles. The Greek word *thlipsis* (pronounced "THLIP-sis"), usually translated as "trouble" or "affliction" in 2 Corinthians 1:4, is related to the verb *thlibō* (pronounced "THLEE-boh"), which can refer to the crushing of grapes or the squeezing of something under pressure. In such moments, God offers his children assurance: "You are not alone; the Holy Spirit is with you." Whether or not you feel his presence, cling to this truth—you will experience consolation. If not immediately, then soon.

The Holy Spirit consoles believers not only for their own sake, but also for the sake of others. Paul puts it this way: "He comforts [consoles] us in all our troubles so that we can comfort [console] others. When they are troubled, we will be able to give them the same comfort [consolation] God has given us" (2 Corinthians 1:4, NLT). As Ferdinand Mount might put it, God's "great generosity" calls those who follow Christ to extend generous consolation to others in their moments of trial.

Likewise, the author of the Peace Prayer seeks to become more like Jesus by coming alongside those who are suffering to offer compassion and relief. Paul shows the same desire to care for others when he writes, "For just as we share abundantly in the sufferings of Christ, so also our comfort [consolation] abounds through Christ. If we are distressed, it is for your comfort [consolation] and salvation; if we are comforted [consoled], it is for your comfort [consolation], which produces in you patient endurance of the same sufferings we suffer" (2 Corinthians 1:5-6).

RESTORE BEAUTY

It's important to acknowledge that pain has a purpose. It did for Christ, it does for us, and it will for others—when we acknowledge the power of redemption.

Consider the Japanese art of *kintsugi* (also known as *kintsukuroi*), which literally means "golden joinery." When a piece of pottery breaks, the artist repairs it by filling the cracks with lacquer mixed with powdered gold. Rather than hiding the flaws, kintsugi highlights them, transforming what was broken into something uniquely beautiful. The philosophy behind this practice affirms that imperfections are part of an object's history and contribute to its value.

In the same way, our trials and struggles often leave marks—visible or not. But through Christ's redemptive work, those "cracks" are filled with his grace, mercy, and love. Far from diminishing us, they become part of a renewed and more meaningful testimony. As Jesus said to Paul: "My grace is sufficient for you, for my power is made perfect in weakness" (2 Corinthians 12:9).

You may have been broken by pain or trauma. Yet like kintsugi, the cracks that remain can bring added beauty, meaning, and value to your life. These marks—like those on Christ's own body—are now filled with his grace. Your story is one of transformation and renewal. That story can console broken hearts and help restore joy.

As much as anyone I know, Linda is a living work of kintsugi. Through her pregnancy, our daughter's death, and the hope of reunion one day in heaven, Linda has lived what she's learned in her walk with Jesus, finding peace and consolation in him. In so doing, she continues to offer comfort to others who have endured the tragic loss of a child.

Journalist Steve Brawner wrote in the *Times Record*:

> [Linda] DeYmaz . . . has spent a big part of the past 18 years thinking about grief and helping others deal with its effects. Her daughter's stillborn birth in 1995 led her a year later to write *Mommy, Please Don't Cry*. . . . The book in turn made her a trusted counselor for grieving families through the years.[10]

Linda believes grief is a journey, not a destination. She recalls how, weeks after losing Ali Grace, the cards and condolences stopped coming, while her grief remained. Her conviction that Ali Grace is in heaven sustained her and shaped our family's narrative.

Linda's message is clear: "The greatest gift that we can give [grieving] families, that we can give anybody that we know, is to keep that memory alive."[11] Through her writing and compassionate counsel, Linda continues to extend this gift to countless others, offering comfort from the heart of her own sorrow.

RESPOND TO PAIN

In this broken world, suffering is unavoidable. Yet how we respond to others in grief reveals the depth of our humanity and faith. For those who desire to become more like Jesus, suffering presents a profound invitation to embody his compassion, enter into the pain of others, and participate in the work of redemption.

Hard as it may be, leaning into the pain of others reflects true compassion, offers consolation, and gently moves them toward healing. Christ doesn't call us to console from a distance but to embody his presence and trust him to work through us. In such moments, our own scars become vessels of grace, filled with beauty, meaning, and value because of his redemptive work. They bear witness to those we encounter that restoration and healing is truly possible.

Having received consolation, we are called to extend it to others as instruments of peace, so that Jesus may restore beauty from brokenness in their lives as well.

QUESTIONS FOR REFLECTION

1. Reflect on a time when you were consoled by someone. What did that person do or say that helped most?
2. What fears or hesitations keep you from walking alongside others in their grief or suffering? How might you overcome them?
3. When others need consolation, how can you be present for them in meaningful ways? Given your own personality, gifts, or experiences, what can you offer to them?

CHAPTER 10

Try to Understand

Grant that I may not so much seek to be understood as to understand.

Mosaic is located in the heart of Little Rock's urban core, adjacent to Fourche Creek, where many unsheltered neighbors live in makeshift camps along the water's edge. When heavy storms pass through, the creek floods—washing away tents, belongings, and what little stability they have, forcing them to start over.

Although the church is already deeply engaged throughout the week in serving this at-risk population, making permanent housing available to them would be transformative.

With this in mind, a group of successful business leaders and entrepreneurs from Mosaic gathered with our executive team in 2023 to consider a nearby 32,000-square-foot building that had recently been listed for lease. Rather than renting the two-story former medical clinic and pharmacy, however, we hoped to acquire the facility outright. If so, we could renovate the second floor for housing while leasing out the ground level to generate income and help offset expenses.

After our team presented what we knew about the building, the group affirmed both the need and the opportunity. They then offered valuable financial insight. While we believed $1 million was a fair purchase price, they estimated the property's actual value to be closer to $500,000. Even with two committed tenants and an estimated $7,000 in monthly rental income, they noted that the building carried an annual property tax burden of more than $100,000. Additionally, at least $800,000 would be required just to restore the HVAC and electrical systems before the building could be put to meaningful use.

In short, the group advised us to set the dream aside for now, trusting that if God truly intends for us to own the building, the opportunity will return under more favorable conditions.[1]

When it comes to money, I learned a long time ago: There's a fine line between faith and foolishness. Instead of pressing the group to agree, then, our team gained understanding by listening first and yielding to collective wisdom. As a result, the advisory group refocused our attention to further developing our existing facility, and likely spared the church unforeseen difficulties. Though setting aside our vision was hard, it was the right decision.

LISTEN WELL

Sadly, it has become both normal and expected in our culture to speak before we listen, and to declare opinions rather than consider perspectives different from our own. The internet and social media give us unprecedented reach, yet they also reward the loudest, most provocative voices. The result is a culture that prizes visibility over vulnerability, rhetoric over reflection, and reaction over relationship.

This has profoundly affected our society. Public discourse grows more polarized with opposing viewpoints reduced to sound bites and caricatures. Empathy and curiosity give way to tribalism and defensiveness. The art of listening has been devalued, leaving many feeling unheard, unseen, and disconnected, despite having more ways to communicate than ever before.

Unsurprisingly, outrage has become a default response to disagreement—both in public discourse and in personal relationships. Reactive outbursts are especially difficult to restrain when we're on the receiving end of injustice, rejection, or a broken agreement. In such moments, the desire to be heard can easily give way to a desire to win. When dominance, rather than understanding, becomes the goal, trust erodes, divisions deepen, and people retreat into echo chambers that only reinforce their existing biases.

In contrast, the apostle James exhorts believers to "be quick to hear, slow to speak, and slow to anger" (James 1:19, NASB). His counsel is good—a recipe for becoming instruments of peace. By modeling those attitudes and seeking to understand rather than to be understood, we help rebuild bridges of empathy and restore a sense of shared humanity.

According to 1 Kings 4:29, "God gave Solomon wisdom and very great insight, and a breadth of understanding as measureless as the sand on the seashore." So when it comes to understanding, we should trust his advice: "The beginning of wisdom is this: Get wisdom. Though it cost all you have, get understanding" (Proverbs 4:7).

The Hebrew word used here for "understanding" is *binah* (pronounced "bee-NAH"), which often means "discernment."[2] In a sermon at Mosaic on the topic, Lawrence Hicks explained that understanding is more than just hearing what someone says. The

English word combines "under" and "stand," suggesting that we need to "stand under" others in order to truly comprehend them. This means approaching others with humility, quieting our minds, and looking beyond the surface of someone else's words to understand the experiences that shape their views.[3]

By contrast, when we speak without considering how our words might be received—or assume others will naturally understand and agree with our intentions—we risk causing unintended harm. Failure to do so often leads to misunderstanding, interpersonal conflict, or even cancellation. To avoid these pitfalls and become instruments of peace, we must discipline our minds, guard our tongues, and engage others—whether in person or online—with growing thoughtfulness and care.

LEARN MUCH

The unnamed author of an article published by the Ford Foundation writes, "Some people may hear 'listen' as synonymous with 'stop talking.' But listening is not a passive act of staying quiet; it's an active choice to engage with others, and to be critical and compassionate in equal measure."[4] The writer observes, "As I've found through many of these conversations in my own life, you don't have to change your position to change your perspective. I've never regretted giving listening a chance. Every time, I've learned something new."[5]

Describing additional benefits of listening, the article continues, "Listening gives meaning to speech, gives purpose to voice, and gives dignity to people. Otherwise, it's just talk. Only when we listen can we find common ground. Only when we listen can we forge compromise and a common future. And only when we listen can we begin to heal the divides throughout this country, and build the bridges that our democracy today so desperately needs."[6] As the author reminds us, true understanding requires thoughtful, active listening—especially when we're engaging with voices that challenge or offend us.

I've always believed that while no one is right about everything, everyone is right about something. With that in mind—and to truly "give listening a chance"—we might ask ourselves, especially in moments of disagreement or their aftermath: *What is this person saying, experiencing, or advocating that is true, valid, or worthy of deeper reflection?*

Once we gain understanding, any response—whether we agree or not—should aim to reflect "peace, goodwill toward men" (Luke 2:14, NKJV). While I fully support free speech, I also believe that whatever we say as Christians should represent Jesus well and, by extension, the churches we attend.

Consider that ambassadors of earthly nations don't speak for themselves or act on personal impulse. They are not even permitted to do so. Instead, they are required to represent the one who appointed them and advance the interests of their government.

Similarly, we should recognize:

> God was reconciling the world to himself in Christ, not counting people's sins against them. And he has committed to us the message of reconciliation. We are therefore Christ's ambassadors, as though God were making his appeal through us. We implore you on Christ's behalf: Be reconciled to God.
>
> **2 CORINTHIANS 5:19-20**

In other words, those who are made new in Christ are appointed to be his ambassadors. It is our duty to advance the mission of reconciliation on behalf of our King and his Kingdom.[7]

For that reason, it is neither our right nor our role to speak or act on our own authority. While we may care deeply about politicized issues or moral causes—including those rooted in biblical conviction—our ultimate calling is not merely to take sides or advance agendas but to faithfully represent Jesus well. As ambassadors of his Kingdom, we'll need to pursue justice and righteousness in ways that reflect his character and advance his mission of reconciliation. This requires wisdom and discernment, ensuring our words and actions draw people toward Christ rather than push them away. Otherwise, we risk becoming stumbling blocks to those we hope to reach.

MAKE A DIFFERENCE

Driven by frustration, I'm often tempted to counter the world's foolishness with biblical truth. I also feel a pressure to speak out at times from those who insist that "silence is complicity." Even so, I've learned there are many ways to avoid complicity—speaking out is one of them. In fact, I remain convinced that actions speak louder than words, and that tangible impact is more productive than symbolic outrage.

For example, in 2023 Prince William launched the Homewards project—a five-year initiative targeting homelessness in six areas across the United Kingdom.[8] Inspired by his late mother Princess Diana and their visits to shelters during his youth, Prince William emphasized the importance of using his platform to get results beyond rhetoric. At the time, he said, "With my position and my platform, I should be delivering change. Why else would I be here if I'm not using this role properly to help people who are in need?"[9]

To date, the initiative has successfully mobilized local coalitions in its six pilot locations, comprising over seventy organizations and community members.[10] Additional plans were announced in February 2024 to build twenty-four homes in Nansledan to provide temporary accommodation for individuals experiencing homelessness.[11] Future plans include constructing "400 social rent homes and a further 475 affordable dwellings" southeast of Faversham.[12]

SHIFT THE TONE

Newton's third law of motion states that "for every action, there is an equal and opposite reaction."[13] This same law applies to human relationships as well. The harder one pushes to be understood using argumentative rhetoric, the more others that disagree will push back with similar force in their efforts to be understood.

It doesn't take Newton's genius to recognize that we are drowning today in a polluted sea of people attempting to be seen and heard, and to influence others. Upon reflection, we should recognize that many are seeking more to be understood than to understand. In this environment, those with differing opinions are marginalized, ostracized, or demonized. This is especially true when we lack personal relationships with people of varying color, class, or culture—when implicit bias may be present, or when we fear what the spread of values unlike our own might mean for those we love.

So let me ask: *How's that working for us?*

As the saying goes, "Insanity is doing the same thing over and over again and expecting different results."[14] To break the destructive cycle of animosity and polarization at the bridge of Christ's humanity, it's important not only to get understanding but also to bear the fruit of the Spirit as we interact with those who disagree. Like a skilled television moderator who keeps panelists calm and focused, peacemakers help others pause, rethink, and reframe—injecting humility and wisdom into increasingly heated moments to de-escalate tensions and redirect interactions toward understanding.

Years ago, I addressed the why and how of becoming a peacemaker in an article for *Outreach* magazine titled "Seven Guiding Principles for Advancing Peace."[15] Among the principles I shared at the time, at least three of them are worth repeating:

1. *Assume the best of others.* The goal is not to win arguments but to win others to Christ. To do so, we need to push aside suspicions of another's motives that might cloud or confuse our interaction with them. We should see others as potential friends to be gained through love rather than enemies to be fought and conquered.

2. *Ask good questions.* Many people do not take time to think deeply about their own beliefs or opinions. Before drawing conclusions, we should invite others to help us understand what lies below the surface of their thoughts, words, or actions. We should allow compassion and sensitivity to inform our response. We should speak to the pain and not the issue.

3. *Acknowledge complexities.* Divisive topics divide for a reason. There are no easy answers. Sadly, many people demonstrate an inability to think or speak with nuance. Finding common ground or acknowledging the perspectives of others, even when we don't agree, can help us gain understanding as well as further productive conversations.

MODEL RESPECT

Easter Sunday typically draws the largest crowd of the year in churches throughout the world. That day, pastors and staff craft the entire experience with first-time visitors in mind. The hope is that both guests and occasional attenders will feel genuinely welcomed and soon return, join the church, or more consistently attend in the future. It's generally not a time to take risks—especially those that might be misunderstood or misinterpreted.

Yet we took such a risk at Mosaic one Easter by inviting two longtime lay members of our church to close each service in prayer. As the final song ended and people expected to be dismissed, Joyce Elliott—an African American state senator largely respected as the leading voice among Democrats in Arkansas for nearly twenty years—approached the stage as did Ralph Hudson—a white Republican and former member of Arkansas's House of Representatives.

Standing together, side by side, Joyce said, "Good morning, I'm Joyce Elliott, and I'm a Democrat." Then Ralph said, "Hello, I'm Ralph Hudson, and I'm a Republican."

Now, this took place during Donald J. Trump's first term as president. In that moment, people held their collective breath and wondered, *What in the world is this about . . . and why now, on a day meant to celebrate Christ's resurrection and the hope of the gospel?*

Anticipating such tension and in a spirit of unison, Joyce and Ralph then said, "But don't worry: We love Jesus, we love this church, and we love each other."

Through the years that Joyce and Ralph have worshiped together at Mosaic, they've modeled a unity in Christ that transcends this world's expectations. They've interacted with each other as people of peace. Having been saved by the same God and informed by the same Bible, and as members of the same church, they do not question or doubt each other's motivations. While they don't always agree on policies or methods, they both seek to improve the lives of Arkansans. They model the mission, vision, and values of our church.

Stated another way, Joyce and Ralph respect, understand, and love each other. They share a love for Christ, for Mosaic, and for others with different political opinions. Through the years, they've raised the relevance and respect of Jesus' good name throughout the state. In so doing, they've become instruments of peace.

QUESTIONS FOR REFLECTION

1. What people in your life do you struggle to understand, and why?
2. Put yourself in their shoes: Imagine their past experiences, current circumstances, and real or perceived fears and pain. Upon reflection, are you able to affirm anything they say? Where can you find common ground?

3. Understanding what it's like when others dismiss your thoughts or feelings, how might you advocate for others in similar circumstances in order to represent Jesus well?

CHAPTER 11

Purpose to Love

Grant that I may not so much seek to be loved as to love.

Affirmation . . . attraction . . . admiration . . . affection. These are just a few words that begin to capture the many definitions of *love.* In fact, history is full of poems, songs, paintings, sculptures, books, movies, and other expressions that convey and celebrate "a set of emotions and behaviors characterized by intimacy, passion, and commitment."[1] Our longing to be loved—and to express love romantically, within families, or through compassion—is part of what it means to be human. Even so, science writer Scott Edwards notes, "Love may well be one of the most studied, but least understood, behaviors. More than twenty years ago, the biological anthropologist Helen Fisher studied 166 societies and found evidence of romantic love—the kind that leaves one breathless and euphoric—in 147 of them."[2]

As for our Creator, John writes twice within nine verses, "God is love" (1 John 4:8, 16). In other words, love is intrinsic to who God is, how he acts, and why he relates to us. It's fundamental to his nature. And because we are made in his image, love is intrinsic to us as well.

PRACTICE *AGAPĒ*

God's love is unique. In both verses just mentioned, John uses a specific Greek term to describe divine love: *agapē* (pronounced "ah-GAH-pay"). "Agapē . . . is the kind of love and action that shows empathy; extends the desire for good; wants the best for others . . . offers help or demonstrates beneficial intentions; and is meant for everyone. Agapē love is sacrificial."[3]

There are several other Greek words also translated as "love" in English. One is *philia* (pronounced "fil-EE-ah"), from which the city of Philadelphia—"the City of Brotherly Love"—derives its name. *Philia* expresses the deep bond of friendship, mutual respect, and affection between equals. It's not romantic or unconditional love, but it thrives on connection, loyalty, and shared experience. Bruce Hurt defines *phileō* (the related verb) as "to be a friend to another, fond of an individual or an object."[4] So *philia* centers on friendship and emotional attachment rooted in fondness and devotion.

While *philia* flows from the heart, *agapē* is largely a decision of the will—it chooses to love unconditionally.

Another Greek word, *erōs* (pronounced "EHR-ohs"), refers to romantic or passionate love. It's the root of the word *erotic* and is associated with longing and desire. In contrast, *agapē* is selfless and giving. It expects nothing in return and isn't based on the worthiness of the person being loved. Rather, it makes them worthy through the very act of loving, just as God's love makes us worthy.

Affirming that God is love (*agapē*) is to recognize at least seven things about his character:

1. He is empathetic.
2. He extends hope and wants the best for others.
3. He is helpful and demonstrates good intentions.
4. He is sacrificial.
5. He is unselfish.
6. He brings worth to those who need it.
7. He loves by choice, unconditionally, as an act of his will.

Such understanding becomes a road map for peacemakers who seek more to love than to be loved.

SACRIFICE SELFLESSLY

The why and how of loving others as God loves us is provided in 1 John 4:

> Dear friends, let us love one another, because love is from God, and everyone who loves has been born of God and knows God.
>
> 1 JOHN 4:7, CSB

Here, love stands at the center of our humanity and the Christian life. It's not just an attribute of God; love is the essence of his nature. Likewise, if we claim to know God, our lives should reflect his love. This truth is not abstract, but calls for expression. Because God first loved us, we are called to love others—not merely with words but sacrificially, through tangible acts.

In the context of John's letter, he is primarily addressing the need for Christians to love one another in the church. However, because John also reminds us that God "sent His Son to be the propitiation for our sins" (1 John 4:10, NKJV), it's clear that we are likewise called to love those outside the church—so that they, too, might come to know Jesus.

So John writes, "Everyone who loves has been born of God and knows God" (1 John 4:7, CSB). This means the expectation to love others—both inside and outside the church—not only affirms our salvation but reflects what those born of God know to be the Father's will. In the very next verse, John adds, "The one who does not love does not know [the will of] God" (1 John 4:8, CSB).

By selflessly loving others who do not yet believe in Jesus, we offer a compelling witness to the gospel and help bring peace to the world.

REMAIN CONSISTENT

Because of love, God sent his Son to live among and die for us, that we might be reconciled to him. From him, we learn that love must be demonstrated beyond sentiment or obligation if it's to be experienced as authentic and credible. Even small, consistent acts of love can have a profound impact on people. For example, a written note, helping hand, or timely gesture can help restore someone's sense of dignity.

We also express love by listening deeply to others' stories, empathizing with their struggles, and meeting their immediate needs without expecting anything in return. But love doesn't stop there. Beyond acts of compassion, peacemakers leverage their assets, gifts, and relationships to help others move forward. Rather than simply "giving them a fish" or even "teaching them to fish," peacemakers love others by making introductions and creating opportunities that help them thrive.[5]

John also emphasizes that love is not merely something we do, but a state of being rooted in God:

> No one has ever seen God; if we love one another, God abides in us and his love is perfected in us.
>
> 1 JOHN 4:12, ESV

In this verse, John uses the word *menō* ("abide"; pronounced "MEH-noh"), which conveys the idea of remaining, dwelling, or staying connected. It's like pitching a tent and remaining with someone in the same spot. *Menō* is also used in John 15 to explain that "as the branch cannot bear fruit by itself, unless it abides in the vine, neither can you [bear fruit], unless you abide in me. I am the vine; you are the branches. Whoever abides in me and I in him, he it is that bears much fruit, for apart from me you can do nothing" (John 15:4-5, ESV). As in 1 John 4:12, these verses also express God's intent for Christians to abide in him as he does in us. When we love one another, we feel his presence and experience his blessing.

John writes in the same verse that when we love others, God's love is "perfected" in us. The Greek word here, *teleioō*, (pronounced "teh-lay-AH-oh") means "to complete, accomplish, or fulfill." Loving others, then, not only reflects God's love but also transforms us.

For example, when we forgive someone, we mirror God's forgiveness. Our hearts are softened, our perspective changes, and we become more like Jesus. Similarly, when we serve others in practical ways, we experience the joy and fulfillment of living out God's purposes.

Love can be exhausting when it requires personal or financial sacrifice. To sustain sacrificial love, then, we'll need to abide in him through prayer, reading Scripture, and worship. Abiding in Christ helps us know when to lean in or step back to love others well. Likewise, it keeps us from engaging others inappropriately, obsessively, or in ways that lead to unintended consequences.

ADDRESS FUNDAMENTAL NEEDS

The psalmist writes, "Delight yourself in the Lord, and He will give you the desires of your heart" (Psalm 37:4, NASB). Humanly speaking, these desires can be summed up in two words that describe our fundamental needs: *security* and *significance*.

Our need for relational security is very real. We long to be loved so we can build trusted, strong, and enduring relationships that steady us in various seasons of our lives. Likewise, we need lasting significance, to know that our lives make a difference and matter to others. For this reason, when others express love or appreciation for us, we feel more than secure—we also feel significant.

Since there's nothing wrong with seeking love, security, or significance, we should ask: *How might we best find the love we seek?*

After my collegiate baseball career, I stayed connected to the game for many years, first as a coach to random players, then to my children and their friends.[6] Interestingly, I discovered more about baseball—for example, preparation, technique, and strategy—as a coach than I ever did as a player.

Similarly, for those seeking love, I've found that the best way to discover it is by prioritizing *agapē*, and by helping others do the same.

The Peace Prayer captures the essence of this calling. In the second section, we pray, *Grant that I may not so much seek to be consoled as to console, to be understood as to understand, to be loved as to love.*

This doesn't mean we should suppress our own need for love. God created us with a desire for relational, emotional, and spiritual connection. However, the prayer does challenge us to prioritize sharing love with others over seeking it from them. When we prioritize loving others, our own needs are often met in surprising ways. For instance, empathy and understanding can deepen relationships and create a sense of mutual care. Offering hope or encouragement can inspire gratitude, which strengthens bonds.

Simply put, we become more like Jesus by loving others unconditionally.

LEAVE A LEGACY

Even with faith in Jesus, many of us still struggle with pride, fear, or insecurity that keeps us from fully loving others. We may hesitate to reach out to someone in need because we fear rejection, feel inadequate, or resist forgiving them because we believe they don't deserve it.

To overcome these challenges, we should remember: God loved us while we were still sinners. His love is not based on merit, but entirely on grace. Embracing this truth frees us to love others as he first loved us.

Practically, this might mean

- choosing to forgive, even when it feels unjust;
- responding graciously to someone who has wronged us; or

- offering to meet a need, even if it feels inconvenient or uncomfortable.

Through *agapē*, we experience the essence of God's presence. Loving others unconditionally sets off a ripple effect, inspiring others to do the same. A single act of love can multiply to create an ecosystem of compassionate care within families, churches, workplaces, schools, and beyond.

Consider the life of Lilias Trotter, a pioneering missionary and artist in the late nineteenth and early twentieth centuries.[7] She left behind the comforts of Victorian England—and a promising art career under the mentorship of John Ruskin—to serve in North Africa. Beyond mere words or sentiment, her courageous and sacrificial acts provide for us an example of how to love others in practice.

1. *Listen empathetically.* Lilias immersed herself in the lives of Algerians, particularly women and children, who were often neglected or oppressed. Rather than imposing herself, she listened intently to their stories, seeking to understand their needs and struggles. Her empathetic approach connected with others on a personal level, demonstrating respect for their dignity and traditions. It helped her earn their trust while breaking down cultural and religious barriers.

2. *Speak words of affirmation.* Lilias brought Jesus near to those she served by leveraging her skills as an artist and storyteller. She often painted vivid illustrations of spiritual truth to help the illiterate understand God's love.

Her words and images affirmed their value as individuals created in his image, inspiring them to embrace their worth and purpose. Many came to see themselves as beloved rather than forgotten by their Creator.

3. *Be generous with time and resources.* For more than forty years, Lilias served the people of Algeria, often at great personal cost. She founded community programs that offered education, medical care, and vocational training to women and children. She worked tirelessly to secure resources for meeting physical and spiritual needs, treating illness, teaching literacy, and feeding the poor. Her generosity extended far beyond material assistance; she gave herself fully to the people she served.
4. *Let go of resentment and extend grace.* Lilias faced significant challenges along the way, including hostility from those who opposed her mission and moments when her efforts bore little fruit. Yet she remained faithful, extending grace even when met with skepticism or rejection. She understood that transformation takes time; her persistence encouraged many to persevere in their own journeys.
5. *Be present in times of joy and sorrow.* Lilias was a constant presence in the lives of the Algerian people. She celebrated their joys and mourned with them in their losses. Her presence assured them that they were not alone and their lives mattered. Her willingness to share in their struggles and triumphs reflected the heart of Christ.

6. *Press on through suffering.* Lilias battled significant health challenges, particularly weakness of the heart and chronic illnesses related to physical exhaustion. Her declining health worsened over decades of missionary work due to the harsh climate, demanding needs, and lack of access to advanced medical care. Despite these challenges, she remained committed and pressed on through suffering.

Through these actions, Lilias Trotter demonstrated how practical love can effect profound change. Her legacy reminds us that when we love as God loves—actively—the peace of Christ is brought near to others in need. By incorporating such practices daily, we not only reflect God's love but also fulfill our own need for relational security and lasting significance.

Ultimately, loving others is less about meeting needs and more about representing Jesus well. By loving as he loved, selflessly and sacrificially, we bring peace to the world and fulfill our calling to walk in his anointing. This is the why, how, and what of peacemaking: Abide in the presence of Jesus, engage others at the bridge of Christ's humanity, and in so doing, point them to the bridge of his divinity.

QUESTIONS FOR REFLECTION

1. Who has loved you unconditionally? What did they do to make you feel secure and significant?

2. Christ loved us selflessly and sacrificially, even when we were sinners. How does his example inspire you to love others more purposefully too?

3. Love is a choice more than an emotion. Is there someone you should choose to love? Consider what might hold you back—such as pride, fear, or insecurity. How can you demonstrate love in your daily interactions?

PART 4

Blessed in Christ

CHAPTER 12

Give

For it is in giving that we receive.

The DC-3 touched down on a grassy field carved into the lush terrain of Roatán Bay Island—its only control tower a wooden shack with a tin roof and an old radio antenna.[1] Roads hadn't yet been paved across much of the island, giving the place a raw, undeveloped beauty. That Christmas break, a group of college students and I arrived on a mission hosted by Roatán's then-governor—a devout follower of Christ. Through his hospitality, we were invited to encourage local believers and help construct a cinder block church in the heart of Coxen Hole, the island's bustling main town.

One day, I noticed a little boy—maybe five years old—kicking around a weather-worn soccer ball. It was an opportunity to break from slinging cinder blocks, so I joined him. We passed the ball back and forth in a small patch of open space near the construction site. Soon, a few more children joined us. Before long, the area was too cramped for all the energy. So I moved the growing group to a larger space down the road.

But the children kept coming . . . dozens of them! A local woman then suggested we relocate to a nearby school with a spacious courtyard. Picking up the ball, and holding it over my head so that all the children could clearly see it, I led the way. More kids joined the procession as we walked down the town's main road. They hung on my back, clung to my sides, and swatted playfully at the ball. In the moment, I thought, *This is what Jesus must have felt like when the crowds pressed into him!*

By the time we reached the schoolyard, more than a hundred children were with me. Thankfully, others from our team arrived with more soccer balls, and we set up a spontaneous tournament with makeshift goals and prizes. More than that, we shared our love for Christ with the entire audience, and that day a number of children came to believe in Jesus.

Now, forty years later, I still remember that moment—not just for what we did, but for what I discovered in the process. I had expected to give my time to construction. What I hadn't expected was that God would use my background in sports to connect with children and point them to Jesus. For the first time, I poured myself out in service and, in doing so, discovered the joy of living for Christ. In giving, I received something far greater in return: the gift of a vocational calling.

CULTIVATE A GIVING HEART

At the core of who God is, we find a giving heart. In the beginning, he gave light to the world, breath to Adam, and life to all creation. Today, he continues his acts of giving, offering strength and peace to his people.

Jesus is a giving God and gave his life "for our sins to rescue us from the present evil age" (Galatians 1:4). He also gave us the Holy Spirit, saying, "I will ask the Father, and he will give you another advocate to help you . . . the Holy Spirit, whom the Father will send in my name" (John 14:16, 26). According to the Niceno-Constantinopolitan Creed, the Holy Spirit "proceeds from the Father and the Son, and with the Father and the Son he is worshiped and glorified."[2] Among other things, the Holy Spirit gives us understanding, consolation, guidance, and spiritual gifts.

Simply put, our Triune God gives because it is inherent in his nature. More than that, God gives because he loves us, as we read in what is perhaps the most well-known verse of the Bible: "God so loved the world that he gave his one and only Son" (John 3:16). Paul also writes in Romans: "God demonstrates his own love for us in this: While we were still sinners, Christ died for us" (5:8). In essence, God gives because it's who he is and how he loves.

Having been created in God's image, we find the impulse to give woven into the fabric of our being. Giving is part of what makes us human. We are meant to bless others since God blesses us. As he said to Abram, "I will bless you . . . and all peoples on earth will be blessed through you" (Genesis 12:2-3). Abram first gave himself to God, then was blessed by God, and in turn became a blessing to all.

The degree to which we give reflects the depth of our gratitude for the security, significance, and salvation Jesus has given us.[3] The more we recognize what Christ has done, the more freely we give to others. By grace, he gives us what we don't deserve; by mercy, he withholds what we do deserve. With this in mind, it's only right for us to extend this same grace and mercy to others. As

Jesus said, "From everyone who has been given much, much will be demanded" (Luke 12:48, NASB).

Yet while we're grateful to receive these gifts, we can still be slow to offer them to others. Just as we've received grace and mercy, so we should be quick to affirm and forgive. Any refusal to extend what we've been given is, at best, an oversight—and at worst, hypocrisy. After all, Jesus commanded in Luke 6:37-38:

- "Do not judge, and you will not be judged."
- "Do not condemn, and you will not be condemned."
- "Forgive, and you will be forgiven."
- "Give, and it will be given to you."

SET ASIDE EXPECTATIONS

Most of us naturally give to those closest to us. That's a good thing, but it's only the beginning. Jesus expects us also to give to those we find difficult to love, even our enemies about whom he says, "Do good to them, and lend to them without expecting to get anything back" (Luke 6:35). It's a high standard, for sure; but attached is a powerful promise: "Then your reward will be great, and you will be children of the Most High."

Consider the story of the Good Samaritan in Luke 10:30-35. Jewish leaders looked down on Samaritans, viewing them as people who had corrupted bloodlines through intermarriage and diluted worship practices.[4] Despite these prevailing attitudes, the Samaritan gave himself sacrificially to the Jewish man by bandaging his wounds, taking him to safety, and paying for his care. He didn't stop to think about whether the man deserved it, or if the man would thank or repay him. He simply met the need, gave from his heart, and shared his resources.

This is the kind of sacrifice Jesus calls us to make: giving to others regardless of earthly distinctions. After all, God didn't wait for us to agree with him or prove ourselves worthy of his love. Rather, "while we were still sinners, Christ died for us" (Romans 5:8).

As followers of Jesus and beneficiaries of God's good gifts, we are uniquely poised to give graciously to others who might not deserve our help or whom we find hard to love. We can bring peace to those who don't share our religious or political views or who come from different ethnic, economic, or cultural backgrounds. By doing so, we will represent Jesus well at the bridge of his humanity and separate ourselves from the world's rhetoric and vitriol. To become a peacemaker is to understand that "a gentle answer deflects anger, but harsh words make tempers flare" (Proverbs 15:1, NLT).

Giving to others without distinction or expectation is no easy task. Our natural instinct is often to react in the flesh—especially when faced with difference—rather than respond in the Spirit. Yet as followers of Christ, we are called to rise above such tendencies and live out our supernatural identity as peacemakers. Let's be quick to acknowledge our mistakes when we fall short, apologize sincerely, and seek reconciliation.

GIVE GENEROUSLY

Building on his call to give freely and without expecting anything in return, Jesus goes on to say: "For with the measure you use, it will be measured to you" (Luke 6:38). In other words, the way we treat others ultimately comes back to us. When we choose to forgive and give generously—even to those who are difficult to love—we not only advance peace but also position ourselves to receive God's abundant favor.

In a recent message, Harry asked our congregation a powerful question: *In what measure do you give to others?*[5] He then offered a memorable illustration, linking household measuring tools to different giving mindsets:

- *a teaspoon* (one who gives sparingly): "Sure, I'll give a little something but on my own terms."
- *a cup* (one who gives conditionally): "Sure, I'll give you something but only because you deserve it or so you'll owe me."
- *a bucket* (one who gives liberally): "I'm happy to give you something more than you're expecting; I want nothing in return."

Admittedly, it can be difficult to give generously—with a "bucket" mindset. It often requires us to set aside our own convenience, pride, or fear of loss. But when we do, we reflect God's generosity and make space for him to work through us in others' lives.

Giving isn't just about money. It's about offering whatever we have to meet a need. Sometimes, the gift is tangible: sharing a meal, donating clothing, or providing another form of assistance. Other times, it's emotional or relational: reaching out to someone struggling, connecting individuals to one another, or weeping with those who weep. There is even the gift of time: slowing down to really listen, visiting someone in the hospital, or grocery shopping for a mother grieving the loss of her child. Whatever we give—time, resources, forgiveness, or encouragement—it matters.

Consider the story of a single mother who had recently lost her job. She didn't need advice or a lecture—just someone to sit quietly and listen to her fears and frustrations. A friend took the time to do just that, and it made all the difference. "That was the first time I'd felt seen in weeks," she later said.

According to the Bible, at least twelve ways to approach our giving should be our guide:

1. secretly (Matthew 6:4)
2. freely (Matthew 10:8)
3. joyfully (Luke 7:36-38, 44-48)
4. sacrificially (Mark 12:41-44; Hebrews 13:16)
5. unconditionally (Luke 6:30)
6. generously (2 Corinthians 9:6; 1 Timothy 6:17-18)
7. purposefully (2 Corinthians 9:7)
8. cheerfully (2 Corinthians 9:7)
9. practically (James 2:15-17)
10. to make amends (Luke 19:8)
11. out of poverty or affliction (Luke 21:1-4; 2 Corinthians 8:1-5)
12. with a pure heart and right motive (1 Corinthians 13:3)

Governed by these attitudes and values, we can offer ourselves and our resources to serve God's purposes and reflect his glory.

WALK IN BLESSING

The beauty of giving is that it's never a one-way street. Jesus said, "Give, and it will be given to you. A good measure, pressed down, shaken together and running over, will be poured into your lap"

(Luke 6:38). This doesn't mean we give in order to receive. But it does mean that our giving opens us to blessings we might never have expected.

When we give, we often experience unexpected blessings such as these:

- *Joy.* Giving brings deep satisfaction and affirms our longing for significance.
- *Connection.* Giving builds meaningful relationships—with family, friends, like-minded people, and even strangers.
- *Growth.* Giving stretches our faith and reminds us to rely on God.
- *Purpose.* Giving connects us to something greater than ourselves.

Paul speaks to the nature of giving and receiving in his final conversation with the elders of the church at Ephesus. These were people Paul dearly loved, having spent more than two years living and working among them. Knowing he would never see them again, he reminds the elders: "It is more blessed to give than to receive" (Acts 20:35).

Notice what happens next:

> When Paul had finished speaking, he knelt down with all of them and prayed. They all wept as they embraced him and kissed him. What grieved them most was his statement that they would never see his face again. Then they accompanied him to the ship.
>
> ACTS 20:36-38

Why an embrace of tears? Why their kisses? Why the feeling of grief? Why accompany him to the ship? Paul had given himself to the church at Ephesus. In return, he received the blessings of their respect, appreciation, and love.

Beyond such personal blessings, Scripture highlights at least twelve spiritual and practical benefits of giving:

1. goodness, righteousness, and leaving a lasting legacy (Psalm 112:5-6)
2. our wants and needs will be supplied (Proverbs 3:9-10; Philippians 4:19)
3. the avoidance of ruin (Proverbs 11:24)
4. refreshment (Proverbs 11:25)
5. increased faith (Malachi 3:10)
6. treasure in heaven (Matthew 6:20-21; 1 Timothy 6:18-19)
7. a generous return of abundance and joy (Luke 6:38; 2 Corinthians 9:6-8)
8. joy and happiness (Acts 20:35)
9. abundant blessing in life (2 Corinthians 9:6-8)
10. others will praise God with thanksgiving (2 Corinthians 9:11-13)
11. the prayers of others (2 Corinthians 9:14)
12. Kingdom impact (Philippians 4:14-16)

Considering all that giving produces—both spiritually and practically—we should be more motivated than ever to give ourselves generously to others. Indeed, we risk little in extending grace, mercy, acceptance, and forgiveness. On the contrary, we gain much. Let's not allow fear of loss, ingratitude, or lack of reciprocation to keep us from meeting needs or responding when the Spirit compels us to give.

Harry describes God's giving as a "gigantic wave that crashes over us in moments of our greatest need, when we are desperate for change. God gives when we're caught in addiction, searching for purpose, or looking for love in all the wrong places. In such moments, God should find us highly unacceptable, unforgivable, and unlovable—but on the contrary: When we look to him, God showers us with an ocean's worth of grace, mercy, acceptance, forgiveness, and unconditional love."[6]

To the extent we recognize that we are constantly swimming in an ocean of love, grace, forgiveness, and mercy, we will be moved to invite others into the water—never to block their way to it. Therefore, as peacemakers, we should give gladly, mindful of what God has given us, as the beloved hymn reminds us: "Pardon for sin and a peace that endureth."[7]

QUESTIONS FOR REFLECTION

1. Can you recall when you gave generously—whether financially, emotionally, or through your time—and were unexpectedly blessed in return? What did that experience teach you about the relationship between giving and receiving?

2. What holds you back from being more generous with your money, time, or resources? Are there fears, habits, or assumptions that limit your willingness to give?

3. What are some practical steps you can take to become more generous in your everyday life? This could be through money, time, hospitality, or acts of service.

CHAPTER 13

Pardon

It is in pardoning that we are pardoned.

Pope John Paul II was shot and wounded by Mehmet Ali Ağca on May 13, 1981, while entering St. Peter's Square in Vatican City.[1] The pope was struck twice and suffered significant blood loss but survived. Ağca was apprehended immediately and later sentenced by an Italian court to life in prison.

The attempted assassination shocked the world. Religious leaders are rarely the targets of assassination, and people tend not to forgive or forget such unprovoked aggression. In this instance, faithful followers and even those outside the Roman Catholic Church called for justice. The pope himself would have been well within his rights to press authorities to render the harshest sentence to Ağca within the limits of the law.

But John Paul II was not merely a religious leader or given to retribution. He was an instrument of peace.

Following a remarkable and full recovery, the pope later met and spoke privately with Ağca on December 27, 1983, at the prison where his attacker was held. According to reports at the time, "John Paul tenderly held the hand that had held the gun that was meant to kill him. For 21 minutes, the pope sat with his would-be assassin. . . . The two talked softly. Once or twice, Ağca laughed. The pope forgave him for the shooting. At the end of the meeting, Ağca either kissed the pope's ring or pressed the pope's hand to his forehead in a Muslim gesture of respect."[2]

As Lance Morrow of *Time* magazine reported, "It is difficult to imagine a more perfect economy of drama. The Pope's deed spoke, not his words, and it spoke with the full authority of his mortal life and the danger to which Ağca had subjected it. The meaning of John Paul's forgiveness was profoundly Christian. He embraced his enemy and pardoned him."[3]

Did you catch it?

It wasn't the pope's words but his deed that captured the reporter's attention and that of the world. It was the act of forgiving and embracing someone who had tried to kill him—that is, someone from a different cultural and religious background who did not deserve mercy—that Morrow declared to be "profoundly Christian."

EXPUNGE THE RECORD

Earlier in the Peace Prayer, the author prays for help in forgiving those who offend. But to truly pardon someone often demands something deeper from us.

As mentioned in chapter 4, the word *forgive* "implies that one gives up all claim to [retribution] and to resentment or vengeful feelings."[4] On the other hand, *pardon* "implies that one remits a penalty due for an admitted or established offense"—as in a criminal receiving a pardon and being released from prison or having their record expunged.[5]

So what's the difference between these terms? A pardon is not only personal; it's structural. It fundamentally alters the state of the offender and his or her relationship with the offended. As Paul writes, "I have been crucified with Christ; and it is no longer I who live, but Christ lives in me; and the life which I now live in the flesh I live by faith in the Son of God, who loved me and gave himself up for me" (Galatians 2:20, NASB). Similarly, Paul tells the church at Corinth, "Therefore from now on we recognize no [believer] by the flesh. . . . Therefore if anyone is in Christ, this person is a new creation; the old things passed away; behold, new things have come" (2 Corinthians 5:16-17, NASB).

This is not only the language of forgiveness; it's also the language of pardon.

Jesus spoke this language while dying on the cross, specifically when he addressed one of two convicted criminals crucified alongside him.[6]

> One of the criminals who hung there hurled insults at him: "Aren't you the Messiah? Save yourself and us!"
>
> But the other criminal rebuked him. "Don't you fear God," he said, "since you are under the same sentence? We are punished justly, for we are getting what our deeds deserve. But this man has done nothing wrong."
>
> Then he said, "Jesus, remember me when you come into your kingdom."

> Jesus answered him, "Truly I tell you, today you will be with me in paradise."
>
> LUKE 23:39-43

To become instruments of peace, we, too, must learn to speak the language of pardon.

Theologian William Lane Craig explains that divine forgiveness is more than just God letting go of resentment or bitterness. It is a legal pardon, canceling our liability for punishment. This is not earned; rather, it is given out of God's love and grace. Because of his mercy, God provides the justice required for our sins, allowing us to be fully forgiven.[7] The psalmist also alludes to pardon when he writes, "As far as the east is from the west, so far has he removed our transgressions from us" (Psalm 103:12).

The Hebrew word translated "remove(d)" means "to go or send far away; to become distant."[8] How far away has he sent or removed our transgressions? As far as the east is from the west. How far is that? The distance is incalculable. At any given point, we are always either east of west or west of east—but never moving in both directions at once. Stated another way, the distance between east and west is infinite, as now is the distance between us and our sin, which has been removed as a barrier between God and those who trust him.

In other words:

- If not for pardon, we could not have a relationship with Jesus.
- If not for pardon, we would not have hope.
- If not for pardon, we could not approach him with confidence in prayer (Hebrews 4:16).

- If not for pardon, we would not otherwise be able to stand in the presence of a holy God.

Through initial confession and repentance—when for the first time we embrace Jesus by faith, asking him to be our Lord and Savior—inherited Sin (our sin nature, here identified with a capital *S*) was removed by an act of God made possible by Jesus' death on the cross.[9] He takes away our Sin and cleanses us from all unrighteousness.[10] This is part of what it means to be pardoned or "saved."[11] We are released from Sin's prison. Our record has been expunged.

Because of Christ's love and sacrifice for us, sin no longer separates us from God. The debt has been paid, sin's power over us has been broken, and we are fully pardoned.[12] Because of this, our identity as offenders is fundamentally altered. We are no longer seen as guilty in his sight. We have been crucified with Christ and redeemed by the blood of the Lamb.

ACT IN OBEDIENCE

That said, we are not yet free of our humanity, temptation, or sin. Because we are weak in the flesh, there remains an ongoing need for self-examination, confession, and repentance.[13]

When my children were younger and arguing with each other, I would ask what happened. Inevitably, one of them would share their version of the story, and the other would respond by calling them a liar. In such instances, I would try to explain the difference between being a Liar (capital *L* to indicate intrinsic nature or identity) and telling a lie.

That's how it is for those of us pardoned by God through faith.

We are no longer Liars—though we may still wrestle with lying.

We are no longer Sinners—though we continue to struggle with sin.

So Paul writes, "Walk by the Spirit, and you will not carry out the desire of the flesh" (Galatians 5:16, NASB).

One of the most powerful examples comes from Corrie ten Boom—a Dutch Christian who, with her family, helped many Jews escape the Holocaust. Eventually captured, she endured imprisonment in a brutal concentration camp called Ravensbrück, where she lost her beloved sister, Betsie.

Years later, Corrie spoke at a church in Germany when a man approached her. To her shock, she recognized him as one of the former guards from Ravensbrück—the very place where she had suffered so much and lost her sister. He did not recognize her, but he reached out his hand and said, "I have become a Christian. I know that God has forgiven me for the cruel things I did there, but I would like to hear it from your lips as well. Fraulein, . . . will you forgive me?"[14]

Corrie later wrote that in that moment, everything in her wanted to withhold forgiveness. The memories. The pain. The loss. How could she offer grace to someone who had caused such suffering? But she also remembered Christ's command: "Forgive as the Lord forgave you" (Colossians 3:13). Corrie prayed for strength, and taking his hand, she felt the love of God flow through her. "I forgive you, brother!" she said, "With all my heart."[15]

This act of pardon was not about the guard deserving forgiveness; he didn't. It wasn't about waiting until she felt like forgiving; she didn't. It was an act of obedience offered to God.

REFUSE RETALIATION

As with Corrie ten Boom, we who have received God's pardon from Sin should be quick to forgive and pardon others. By doing so, we release bitterness and free ourselves from the grip of resentment. Pardoning someone is not to excuse wrongdoing, nor do we pretend that wounds don't exist. Instead, we surrender the right to retaliate, refuse to let the past dictate our future, and entrust justice to God.

It's hard enough to pardon someone when they express regret, let alone when they don't seek forgiveness. Nevertheless, even when others do not readily (if ever) acknowledge their actions, apologize to us, or seek reconciliation, we should pardon them for the sake of our own well-being.

If you find it difficult to forgive someone who has never asked for it, remember Jesus' words from the cross: "Father, forgive them, for they do not know what they are doing" (Luke 23:34). These words not only extended peace to those who crucified and mocked him, but also revealed Jesus' unwavering resolve to remain faithful through suffering. It was this very resolve and faithfulness that moved a centurion to declare, "Surely this was a righteous man" (Luke 23:47).

South African Archbishop Desmond Tutu was an anti-apartheid and human rights activist. Speaking of forgiveness (but also appropriate for discussing pardon), he wrote,

> I realize how difficult the process of forgiving truly is. . . . Spiritually, I know my faith tells me [to forgive] as God forgives us all. But it is still difficult. The traumas we have witnessed or experienced live on in our memories. . . .

> It is perfectly normal to want to hurt back when you have been hurt. But hurting back rarely satisfies. We think it will, but it doesn't. . . . Retaliation gives, at best, only momentary respite from our pain. The only way to experience healing and peace is to forgive. . . .
>
> Without forgiveness, we remain tethered to the person who harmed us. We are bound with chains of bitterness, tied together, trapped. Until we can forgive the person who harmed us, that person will hold the keys to our happiness; that person will be our jailor. When we forgive, we take back control of our own fate and our feelings. We become our own liberators. We don't forgive to help the other person. We don't forgive for others. We forgive for ourselves.[16]

LIBERATE SOULS

Another South African, Nelson Mandela, spent twenty-seven years in a jail cell for anti-apartheid activism. For eighteen of those years, he was "confined to a small cell without a bed or plumbing [and] forced to do hard labor in a quarry. He could write and receive a letter once every six months, and once a year he was allowed to meet with a visitor for 30 minutes."[17] In the aftermath of apartheid and four years after being released from prison, Madiba (as he was sometimes called) became South Africa's president. A journalist later observed,

> Certainly, Madiba . . . did not come to forgive his torturers effortlessly. . . . He himself confided that in the first moments after leaving prison, anger was his

predominant feeling. But it was at that key passage in his life (and in the history of South Africa) that, as he recounted, he heard this admonition from the Lord: "Nelson, while you were in prison you were free, now that you are free, don't become their prisoner." Mandela thus decided not to remain trapped in the past, but to let the bitterness go. He was aware, as he later stated, that "Forgiveness liberates the soul. It removes fear. That is why it is such a powerful weapon."[18]

MAKE PEACE AND BUILD

As a form of motivation, the author of the Peace Prayer challenges us to imitate Christ. Extending pardon will require us to release fleshly desires and surrender any thoughts of revenge, retaliation, or retribution. Such things must be cast far from us—as far as the east is from the west. Only then can our hearts be transformed and our lives take a new direction.

Through a deliberate act of the will, we can refuse to remain bound to the hurt, harm, or lingering effects of an offense. Instead of remaining stuck in the past, we can expunge the offender's record and step boldly into a future marked by strength, freedom, and hope. By not only forgiving but pardoning others, we open ourselves to more fully experience the pardon of God—especially after moments or seasons of our own failure.

With forgiveness and pardon in mind, Mandela said, "It is so easy to break down and destroy. The heroes are those who make peace and build."[19] Though difficult, let us follow the example of the heroes and saints of old—those who made peace and built—by choosing to pardon others. In so doing, we become more like Jesus.

QUESTIONS FOR REFLECTION

1. When you think about the truth that Jesus has forgiven you, how does it make you feel? What impact has his mercy and grace had on your life, your relationships, and your view of others?

2. Have you held on to resentment or bitterness toward another person? How do these feelings affect your heart, mind, or relationships? What emotions or fears make it difficult to extend forgiveness?

3. What steps can you take to begin releasing any resentments to embrace forgiveness? Or if someone you know harbors such resentment toward another, how can you help or encourage them to release it?

CHAPTER 14

Flourish

It is in dying that we are born to eternal life.

Sam and Laura were a dynamic young couple who volunteered as youth leaders in their local church and spent a week each summer serving as camp counselors. When Laura became pregnant with their first child, however, doctors discovered a congenital heart defect that could complicate the delivery. Her physician explained there was a significant risk that Laura could die in childbirth—her heart was not strong enough to carry the baby to term, let alone withstand delivery. As a result, he recommended an abortion to save Laura's life.

The news was devastating for the Christ-centered couple. More than that, Sam and Laura faced an excruciating decision: terminate the pregnancy to preserve Laura's life or proceed by faith and entrust the outcome to God.

After much agonizing prayer, Sam and Laura chose to continue the pregnancy. In doing so, they surrendered themselves and their child into the Father's hands, praying as Jesus taught: "Your will be done" (Matthew 6:10).

When the time came to deliver, both mother and child survived—to the prayerful joy of everyone involved. Under intense observation, Laura and her baby made it through like champions. Later, after holding her newborn and celebrating with Sam, Laura praised God for faith's reward and drifted off to sleep.

Tragically, she never woke again.

Sometime during the night, Laura's heart gave out, just as the doctors had feared.

In the days that followed, Sam navigated the emotional extremes of welcoming his newborn daughter and grieving the loss of his beloved wife. During the joy and sorrow, he arranged Laura's funeral and burial. Soon after, he commissioned a headstone engraved with her full name, dates of birth and death, and a phrase the couple had repeated often as they made their difficult choice—an expression of their unwavering faith in Christ:

Some things are worth dying for.

Laura's willingness to die so her child might live is a powerful reflection of Christ's own sacrifice that gave us eternal life. In her moment of both tragedy and triumph, Laura entrusted herself to a faithful Creator, echoing the words of Jesus: "No one takes [my life] from me, but I lay it down of my own accord" (John 10:18). He also said, "Greater love has no one than this: to lay down one's life for one's friends" (John 15:13). Emboldened by faith, Laura demonstrated this greater love by loving her child more than her own life.

KEEP TOMORROW IN MIND

At the end of the Peace Prayer, the author affirms that "it is in dying that we are born to eternal life." With this in mind, a passage in John 12 is both helpful and instructive.

During the final week of his earthly life and after arriving in Jerusalem to celebrate one last Passover with his disciples, Jesus spoke of his impending death:

> "The hour has come for the Son of Man to be glorified. Truly, truly I say to you, unless a grain of wheat falls into the earth and dies, it remains alone; but if it dies, it bears much fruit. The one who loves his life loses it, and the one who hates his life in this world will keep it to eternal life. If anyone serves Me, he must follow Me; and where I am, there My servant will be also; if anyone serves Me, the Father will honor him."
>
> JOHN 12:23-26, NASB

Let's dive deeper into this passage.

First, Jesus says that his hour has come. He knew his death was imminent. For the rest of us, however, the hour of our death remains pending. With that day in mind, the psalmist writes:

> Your eyes have seen my formless substance,
> and in your book were written
> all the days that were ordained for me
> when as yet there was not one of them.
>
> PSALM 139:16, NASB

As we know, an hour is coming and there's no escaping it. All of us will die as God has ordained.

Now nearing sixty-five, I've lived more days than I have left on this earth—and I'll admit, the certainty of death sometimes terrifies me. On more than one occasion I've bolted awake, gripped by the fact that nothing can halt what's coming—the end of my earthly life.

In those moments of anxiety, I find myself wondering things like these:

- *Will my death be painful? . . . I hope not!*
- *Will I die before Linda? And, if so, will she someday give her heart to another?*
- *Will my children and grandchildren remember me with love and gratitude?*
- *Will I live long enough to meet a great-grandchild?*
- *Will what I've pursued for Christ have lasting impact?*
- *Will the church we planted continue to bless and shape our community?*
- *Will I hear Jesus say to me, "Well done, good and faithful servant"?*

All such questioning is human. Simply put, there's nothing wrong with feeling this way about the future from time to time. Even so, we can take heart in biblical truth and in Christ—especially in the courage Jesus displayed as he faced his own death. Rather than fret, he determined to glorify God in and through it. So let's decide, even now, to face our own moment with the same courage and confidence in Christ. By speaking words of faith, peace, and assurance to those we love, we can glorify him in our final hour.

Just as he had done throughout his earthly life, Jesus clung to purpose even in the hour of his death. So he concluded,

> "Father, glorify your name." Then a voice came out of heaven: "I have both glorified it, and will glorify it again."
>
> JOHN 12:28, NASB

I imagine it was just the assurance Jesus needed in the moment to set aside anxious human thoughts and remain confident in death, knowing that there was yet life ahead—and that in dying, he would not only live but give us all eternal life.

PROPAGATE LIFE

To comfort the disciples about his own death, Jesus drew an analogy from nature. He said,

> "Truly, truly I say to you, unless a grain of wheat falls into the earth and dies, it remains alone; but if it dies, it bears much fruit."
>
> JOHN 12:24, NASB

In other words, only when a seed falls can germination begin—a process by which new fruit from the seed is propagated. As Sally Bavin explains, germination begins when the seed dies and transforms: "Once a seed has germinated, the root grows down into the soil to absorb moisture and nutrients and begin to anchor the plant into the ground. At the same time, a green shoot grows up towards the light."[1] What, then, is Christ's point? In nature, the "death" of a seed leads to the birth and spread of life—just as the death of Jesus makes eternal life possible for all who believe in him (Romans 10:9, 13).

But Jesus' analogy pointed to more than a natural process—it conveyed a spiritual truth. In discussing the germination of a seed, he not only spoke of physical life and death but also, in a spiritual sense, of putting to death our own sinful flesh in order to experience the fullness of life he offers.

He added,

> "The one who loves his life loses it, and the one who hates his life in this world will keep it to eternal life."
>
> **JOHN 12:25, NASB**

Paradoxically, the path to abundant life on earth and eternal life in heaven begins by surrendering our will to the will of Christ.

This wasn't the only time Jesus addressed this theme. For example, in the Gospel of Matthew he said,

> "If anyone would come after me, let him deny himself and take up his cross and follow me. For whoever would save his life will lose it, but whoever loses his life for my sake will find it. For what will it profit a man if he gains the whole world and forfeits his soul?"
>
> **MATTHEW 16:24-26, ESV**

Similarly, he said,

> "But seek first the kingdom of God and his righteousness, and all these things will be provided for you."
>
> **MATTHEW 6:33, CSB**

In short, Jesus calls his followers to multiply life by pursuing Kingdom values over worldly ambitions.

GLORIFY GOD

John explains, "This is how we know what love is: Jesus Christ laid down his life for us. And we ought to lay down our lives for our brothers and sisters" (1 John 3:16). Jesus commands us, "Love one another, just as I have loved you" (John 15:12, NASB).

Most of us will never face the choice of sacrificing our lives to save another. However, we can and should love others as Christ loved us. It means patterning our lives after the way Jesus lived.

If we have resources to help but choose to look away, we are not acting in love. First John 3:18 says, "Let us not love with words or speech but with actions and in truth." In other words, true love goes beyond kind words—it acts to make a meaningful difference.

In John 12:26, Jesus links serving and following him with a willingness to surrender our lives. This idea is echoed even more explicitly in Mark 8:34-35, where he defines *discipleship* as denying ourselves and taking up our cross. He promises in John 12:26 that those who serve in this way will be honored by the Father. The word *honor* comes from the Greek *timaō* (pronounced "tee-MAH-oh"), which means to "fix a valuation upon; by implication, to revere," "honor," or "value."[2] God values those who follow Jesus and mirror his life. The Father honors those who identify with Christ by becoming peacemakers.

To be more like Jesus, remind yourself of these things each day:

- To know him is to follow him.
- To follow him is to serve him.

- To serve him is to honor him.
- To honor him is to love him.
- To love him is to please him.
- To please him is to identify with him.
- To identify with him is to be a peacemaker.
- To be a peacemaker is to embody the very mission of Christ in a broken world.

FOLLOW HIS EXAMPLE

Hatred, hostility, and division are as old as humanity itself. Indeed, since Cain murdered Abel, humanity has been marked by conflict. What is new is our age of instant communication—where news, opinion, and outrage spread faster than understanding. Ours is a culture marked by polarization, where differences are weaponized, wounds remain untreated, and reconciliation is devalued.

In this age of outrage, the Peace Prayer reminds us that we are called to be instruments of peace. When we inspire love instead of hate, offer pardon over retaliation, bring hope in despair, and seek understanding amid division, we become agents of healing and glorify our Father in heaven. Peace is not forged through louder arguments or deeper entrenchment, but through those committed to walking in Christ's anointing.

As we've seen, peacemaking is not passive—it's a purposeful, active pursuit. It calls us to advocate for justice, love mercy, and walk humbly with others. It also requires patience rooted in faith, courage in the face of opposition, and a willingness to sacrifice. Only then can the Anointed One use us to remove the barriers that keep others from experiencing the *sar shalom*.

Jesus gave his life to bring us peace—with God and with one another. Until our final breath, may we follow his example, die daily to ourselves, and choose to live as instruments of peace.

QUESTIONS FOR REFLECTION

1. What emotions or thoughts arise when you think about physical or spiritual death? How does your faith guide those feelings?
2. What does "dying to yourself" mean to you? Can you recall when surrendering your own desires led to growth, freedom, or deeper faith?
3. How does the promise of eternal life impact the way you engage others today? How does it inspire you to become more like Jesus through peacemaking?

Acknowledgments

It's been over two years since I first envisioned and sensed the need for this book. Now, at last, it's in your hands—made possible by the many good people at NavPress and Tyndale House Publishers.

Special thanks to my friends David Zimmerman (publisher) and Deborah Sáenz (acquisitions and developmental editor) at NavPress. David, thank you for recognizing the importance of this book from the moment I first presented the concept. Deborah, your unwavering belief in the vision and outstanding editorial guidance have made this a far better book than I even imagined. Thank you.

Thanks also to Elizabeth Schroll and Andrew Pottenger for your careful copyediting and to the entire NavPress publishing team for your attention to detail. And to Robin Bermel, Esther Ereneta, Natalie Wierenga, and the Tyndale sales and marketing teams—I'm grateful for your efforts to expand the reach of this important message.

I'm also grateful to David Kinnaman (Barna Group) and Carl McQueen (McQueen Analytics) for their generous time and thoughtful guidance regarding my citation of the *He Gets Us* research.

To my fellow teaching pastors at Mosaic—Harry Li, Lawrence Hicks, and Lauren Carrión: Thank you for helping me shape the VIA series from which this book emerged. Your faithful, sacrificial service to the people of Mosaic and the community we serve is both seen and valued, more than you know.

And to the people of Mosaic Church: Thank you for being the living embodiment of the vision. Your faith, resilience, and determination to walk, work, and worship God together as one—beyond the distinctions of this world that otherwise divide—inspire me daily. This book is, in so many ways, a reflection of your witness. May we continue to be known as a community of peacemakers, representing Jesus well throughout our city and around the world; a church for all people, not just some, on earth as it is in heaven.

Finally, to Linda . . . more than a wife, you are my best friend, most trusted confidante, the one true love of my life—my soulmate. Thank you for your thoughtful engagement with the manuscript in its final stages, which made the book stronger in every way. More importantly, thank you for your steadfast love, unwavering support, and rock-solid faith in Jesus, which, for nearly forty years, has made my life complete and given me far more than I deserve.

Notes

CHAPTER 1 | REPRESENT JESUS WELL

1. Learn more about the *He Gets Us* campaign at https://hegetsus.com.
2. BrandHaven, internal research findings for *He Gets Us*, April–July 2021.
3. BrandHaven is a strategic branding and creative messaging agency that partners with bold mission-driven brands seeking to make a meaningful difference in the world. Learn more at https://brandhavenagency.com.
4. BrandHaven, internal research findings for *He Gets Us*, April–July 2021.
5. McQueen Analytics, internal follow-up research findings for *He Gets Us*, presented by Carl McQueen at the Jesus Now Summit, Dallas, TX, December 2023.
6. BrandHaven, *He Gets Us*, April–July 2021.
7. BrandHaven, *He Gets Us*, April–July 2021, and McQueen Analytics, *He Gets Us*, presented by Carl McQueen at the Jesus Now Summit, Dallas, TX, December 2023.
8. Barna Group, October 21–31, 2022.
9. Barna Group, October 21–31, 2022.
10. BrandHaven, *He Gets Us*, April–July 2021, and McQueen Analytics, *He Gets Us*, presented by Carl McQueen at the Jesus Now Summit, Dallas, TX, December 2023.
11. BrandHaven, *He Gets Us*, April–July 2021.
12. BrandHaven, *He Gets Us*, April–July 2021.
13. If "the bridge of Christ's divinity" invites people to believe in his identity as Lord and Savior, then "the bridge of Christ's humanity" invites them to encounter his compassion, humility, and care.
14. Bill Bright, *The Four Spiritual Laws* (Campus Crusade for Christ, 1965), https://firstpriority.club/wp-content/uploads/2015/10/Four-spiritual-laws.pdf; "What Is the Romans Road to Salvation?," accessed August 15, 2025, https://www.gotquestions.org/Romans-road-salvation.html.

15. My thoughts here are adapted from Mark DeYmaz, "Disrupting Church Economics: Innovating Sustainable Funding for the Future," in *Red Skies: 10 Essential Conversations Exploring Our Future as the Church* (100 Movements Publishing, 2022), 171–190.
16. "Blessed are the peacemakers, for they will be called children of God" (Matthew 5:9).
17. The Van, "I am asked at least once a week how many churches are involved in this work," Facebook, March 17, 2024, https://www.facebook.com/ItsTheVan.

CHAPTER 2 | REFLECT HIS ANOINTING

1. A rectory is a residence where priests live and carry out their pastoral and community responsibilities, often attached to a parish church or educational institution.
2. See www.brophyprep.org.
3. The first stage of Jesuit formation involves "a two-year novitiate where the novice learns about life in the Society of Jesus and begins to live vows of poverty, chastity, and obedience in a community setting," "Jesuit Formation," accessed June 4, 2025, www.jesuitscentralsouthern.org/become-a-jesuit/jesuit-formation.
4. What was then Scottsdale Baptist Church (affiliated at the time with the Conservative Baptist Association of America, now Venture Church Network) is today New Life Community Church, a multiethnic church. Visit www.newlifescottsdale.org.
5. "Peace Prayer," Loyola Press, accessed May 28, 2025, www.loyolapress.com/catholic-resources/prayer/traditional-catholic-prayers/saints-prayers/peace-prayer-of-saint-francis.
6. Kevin Flannagan, "History of Hymns: 'Make Me a Channel of Your Peace,'" June 5, 2018, www.umcdiscipleship.org/resources/history-of-hymns-make-me-a-channel-of-your-peace.
7. See John Barton and John Muddiman, eds., *The Oxford Bible Commentary* (Oxford University Press, 2001), 433–434.
8. Blue Letter Bible, "Lexicon: Strong's H4886—*māšaḥ*," accessed May 14, 2025, https://www.blueletterbible.org/lexicon/h4886/nasb20/wlc/0-1.
9. Further attestations that Jesus is the Christ come from Matthew, who writes that following the temptation of Jesus in the wilderness and after learning "that John [the Baptist] had been put in prison, [Jesus] withdrew to Galilee. Leaving Nazareth [that is, after he identified himself as the Anointed One of Isaiah 61 in the synagogue at Nazareth], he went and lived in Capernaum [another town in Galilee], which was by the lake [i.e., on the northwestern shore of the Sea of Galilee] in the area of Zebulun and Naphtali—to fulfill what was said through the prophet Isaiah: 'Land of Zebulun and land of Naphtali, the Way of the Sea, beyond the Jordan, Galilee of the Gentiles—the people living in darkness have seen a great light; on those living in the land of the shadow of death a light has

dawned.' From that time on Jesus began to preach, 'Repent, for the Kingdom of heaven has come near'" (Matthew 4:12-17).

10. Nazareth was a southern town in Galilee, just north of Samaria's border.
11. At the time of Jesus, participation in discussions and teaching in the synagogue was not limited based on social status or occupation. Rather, individuals with a deep understanding of the Scriptures and religious teachings were often the ones leading discussions and providing commentary on the scrolls. See Alfred Edersheim, *The Life and Times of Jesus the Messiah*, vol. I, new American ed. (E. R. Herrick & Co., 1883), 445–450.
12. We can summarize the latter part of Luke's argument this way: Luke 3:21-38 (paternal genealogy): Luke identifies Jesus as the Son of God; Luke 4:1-13 (temptation in the wilderness): Satan challenges the idea that Jesus is the Son of God; Luke 4:14-21 (pronouncement in the synagogue): Jesus self-identifies as the Anointed One of Isaiah 61.
13. According to the *Brown-Driver-Briggs Hebrew and English Lexicon*, the Hebrew word for peace (*shalom*) encompasses "completeness, soundness, welfare, peace." This includes notions of completeness in number; safety; soundness in body; welfare, health, prosperity; tranquility, contentment; and peace in human relationships and with God, especially in a covenant relationship. See Francis Brown, S. R. Driver, and Charles A. Briggs, *The Brown-Driver-Briggs Hebrew and English Lexicon* (Hendrickson, 1996), s.v. "שָׁלוֹם (*shalom*)." The New Testament Greek word often rendered "peace," *eirenē*, is defined in *Thayer's Greek Lexicon* as "a state of national tranquility"; "peace between individuals, i.e., harmony, concord"; "security, safety, prosperity, felicity"; "the tranquil state of a soul assured of its salvation through Christ and so fearing nothing from God and content with its earthly lot." See Joseph H. Thayer, *Thayer's Greek–English Lexicon of the New Testament* (Hendrickson, 1995), s.v. "*εἰρήνη* (*eirene*)."
14. Mark DeYmaz, *Disruption: Repurposing the Church to Redeem the Community* (Thomas Nelson, 2017), 172.

CHAPTER 3 | SPREAD LOVE

1. "Messianic Jews are lineally Jewish people that believe that Yeshua (Jesus) fulfilled prophecies in the Scriptures." Messianic Jewish Alliance of America, "Who We Are," accessed July 24, 2024, https://mjaa.org/about-us.
2. The American Civil Liberties Union (ACLU) of Arkansas. Learn more at www.acluarkansas.org.
3. Robert Coles, *The Story of Ruby Bridges* (Scholastic, 1995), mentioned in Kim Reisman, "Courage, Will and Freedom," World Methodist Evangelism, March 21, 2024, https://worldmethodist.org/courage-will-and-freedom.
4. Blue Letter Bible, "Lexicon: Strong's H7195—*qešer*," accessed July 9, 2025, https://www.blueletterbible.org/lexicon/h7195/kjv/wlc/0-1.

5. Blue Letter Bible, "Lexicon: Strong's H7194—*qāšar*," accessed May 14, 2025, www.blueletterbible.org/lexicon/h7194/esv/wlc/0-1.
6. Dr. Harry Li is the senior pastor of Mosaic Church in Little Rock, AR. See his sermon on sowing love, not hate, at "VIA: Becoming an Instrument of Peace," sermon by Harry Li, recorded January 21, 2024, Mosaic Church of Central Arkansas, MosaicChurchMedia, YouTube, 33 min., 33 sec., https://www.youtube.com/watch?v=uffBOfsm0ok.
7. Blue Letter Bible, "Lexicon: Strong's G2190—*echthros*," accessed July 3, 2024, www.blueletterbible.org/lexicon/g2190/esv/mgnt/0-1.
8. Exodus 21:23-25 reads, "But if there is serious injury, you are to take life for life, eye for eye, tooth for tooth, hand for hand, foot for foot, burn for burn, wound for wound, bruise for bruise." This same expression ("an eye for an eye") is later repeated in Leviticus 24:20 and Deuteronomy 19:21. Coupled with the passionate appeals to God from David leveled against enemies in times of trial (see Psalm 59:1-5) as well as against those he deems to be enemies of God (Psalm 139:21-22), the notion that God sanctioned the hatred of enemies was an erroneous one, as shown in Matthew 5:43-48.
9. Blue Letter Bible, "Lexicon: Strong's G25—*agapao*," accessed July 19, 2025, https://www.blueletterbible.org/lexicon/g25/niv/mgnt/0-1.

CHAPTER 4 | EXTEND FORGIVENESS

1. *Merriam-Webster Dictionary*, see synonym chooser for "pardon," accessed August 19, 2025, https://www.merriam-webster.com/dictionary/pardon.
2. *Merriam-Webster Dictionary*, see synonym chooser for "forgive," accessed May 15, 2025, https://www.merriam-webster.com/dictionary/forgive.
3. Here's my understanding of these terms: *Grace* is experienced in God giving to us what we don't deserve, while *mercy* is experienced through God withholding from us what we do deserve.
4. An increasingly popular form of bullying today is labeled cyberbullying. "Cyberbullying occurs when someone uses technology to demean, inflict harm, or cause pain to another person." Ashley Abramson, "Cyberbullying: What Is It and How Can You Stop It?," American Psychological Association, September 7, 2022, www.apa.org/topics/bullying/cyberbullying-online-social-media.
5. Ron Marrs, "The Beauty of Two NT Greek Words for Forgiveness," Western Seminary, February 1, 2023, https://transform.westernseminary.edu/resources/the-beauty-of-two-nt-greek-words-for-forgiveness.
6. Ron Marrs, "The Beauty of Two NT Greek Words."
7. Liddell and Scott, *A Greek–English Lexicon*, via Perseus Digital Library, accessed May 31, 2025, https://www.perseus.tufts.edu/hopper//morph?l=a%29%2Ffes&la=greek#lexicon.
8. Marrs, "Beauty of Two NT Greek Words," WesternSeminary.edu.

9. Stanisław Głaz, "The Relationship of Forgiveness and Values with Meaning in Life of Polish Students," *Journal of Religion and Health* 58, no. 5 (October 2019): 1886–1907, www.ncbi.nlm.nih.gov/pmc/articles/PMC6759669.
10. *Merriam-Webster Dictionary*, "ad majorem Dei gloriam," accessed October 14, 2025, www.merriam-webster.com/dictionary/ad%20majorem%20Dei%20gloriam.
11. While a precise print source is not confirmed, the quote is commonly attributed to Billy Graham in various sermons, public reflections, and message excerpts in the voice of Billy Graham, such as "The Closer You Get to Christ, the More Sinful You're Going to Feel," YouTube video, posted by the Billy Graham Evangelistic Association of Canada, accessed July 6, 2024, www.facebook.com/reel/1026016502208098.

CHAPTER 5 | INSPIRE FAITH

1. Learn more about this desert region in ancient Israel at www.britannica.com/place/Negev.
2. "Canaan, a Small Territory Surrounded by Great Empires," The Map as History, accessed March 18, 2024, www.the-map-as-history.com/bible-and-history/canaan-a-small-territory-surrounded-by-great-empires.
3. *Merriam-Webster Dictionary*, "doubt," accessed March 18, 2024, www.merriam-webster.com/dictionary/doubt.
4. *Merriam-Webster Dictionary*, "faith," accessed March 18, 2024, www.merriam-webster.com/dictionary/faith.
5. Quoted by Mark A. Riccobono, "The Understanding of Fear and the Power of Progress," convention address to the National Confederation of the Blind, July 5, 2016, Orlando, Florida, bit.ly/4dcoTBD.
6. Riccobono, "Understanding of Fear," July 5, 2016.
7. In 2005, *Christianity Today* referred to our fledgling church plant as a "Big Dream in Little Rock." John W. Kennedy, "Big Dream in Little Rock," *Christianity Today*, April 2005, https://www.christianitytoday.com/ct/2005/april/24.42.html.

CHAPTER 6 | CULTIVATE HOPE

1. Islapedia, "Chadwick, Florence," updated August 31, 2022, www.islapedia.com/index.php?title=CHADWICK,_Florence.
2. The quote is commonly attributed to author Hal Lindsey; however, a direct source from his published works has not been identified.
3. "Mental Illness," National Institute of Mental Health, updated September 2024, https://www.nimh.nih.gov/health/statistics/mental-illness.
4. Blue Letter Bible, "Lexicon: Strong's G1680—*elpis*," accessed May 29, 2025, https://www.blueletterbible.org/lexicon/g1680/kjv/tr/0-1.

5. *Mommy, Please Don't Cry* is a certified bestseller with well over 150,000 copies sold since it was first published in 1996. It was one of the very first books to address the grief of child loss from a Christian perspective and helped open the door for what is today a recognized literary genre.
6. Blue Letter Bible, "Lexicon: Strong's H6960—*qāvâ*," accessed May 15, 2025, https://www.blueletterbible.org/lexicon/h6960/nasb20/wlc/0-1.
7. Erwin W. Lutzer, "Hope in the Midst of Despair," Moody Church Media, June 19, 2020, www.moodymedia.org/blog/2020/06/why-can-we-have-hope.

CHAPTER 7 | SHINE LIGHT

1. This quote is widely attributed to Brennan Manning and was popularized by its inclusion at the beginning of DC Talk's 1995 song "What If I Stumble?" from the album *Jesus Freak* (ForeFront Records, 1995). While the quote is commonly associated with Manning, a direct citation from his published works has not been identified.
2. Beyond God's "general revelation" of himself in Creation, he has more specifically revealed himself to humankind through his Son, Jesus Christ, and the written Word. This "special revelation" invites people to respond to God in faith—"Anyone who comes to him must believe that he exists and that he rewards those who earnestly seek him" (Hebrews 11:6).
3. This is a more accurate English translation of the phrase than the one otherwise commonly associated with the prayer.
4. In describing us as the light of the world, Jesus is not suggesting that we now stand in equality with him as if having become gods ourselves. Rather, such a description is in keeping with our new identity in Christ (2 Corinthians 5:17). Having been crucified with Christ, "It is no longer I who live but Christ who lives in me" (Galatians 2:20, ESV).
5. This insight was shared with our congregation during a message on the topic of light and darkness. See "VIA: Becoming an Instrument of Peace," sermon by Lawrence Hicks, recorded February 18, 2024, Mosaic Church of Central Arkansas, MosaicChurchMedia, YouTube, 30 min., 4 sec., www.youtube.com/watch?v=CNLHVxfpbGQ&t=1041s.
6. *Accommodate* means "to adjust actions in response to somebody's needs." *Encarta World English Dictionary*, "accommodate," accessed August 20, 2025, https://archive.org/details/encartaworldengl0000unse/page/n5/mode/2up?q=accommodate. *Merriam-Webster* provides a further connotation of the word, namely, "to give consideration to: to allow for"; "to adapt oneself." *Merriam-Webster Dictionary*, "accommodate," accessed May 15, 2025, https://www.merriam-webster.com/dictionary/accommodate. See Mark DeYmaz, *Building a Healthy Multi-Ethnic Church* (Jossey-Bass, 2007), 59.
7. Response to the question "Explain four reasons why you should comport yourself properly," submitted July 19, 2023, by boatengosei024 as part of an

online forum and interaction with others considering the Scholastic Aptitude Test (SAT). https://brainly.com/question/35052509.

8. National Geographic, "Encyclopedic Entry: Photosynthesis," accessed July 26, 2024, https://education.nationalgeographic.org/resource/photosynthesis.
9. Nadjia LaFontaine, "Photosynthesis—The Basis of Life," GreenCover, July 5, 2023, https://greencover.com/photosynthesis-the-basis-of-life.
10. Billy Swan, "Jesus, Photosynthesis, and Redemption," Word on Fire, August 5, 2020, www.wordonfire.org/articles/jesus-photosynthesis-and-redemption.
11. St. John of the Cross, *Dark Night of the Soul*, trans. E. Allison Peers (Image Books, 1959), 100.
12. Karyn Wiseman, "How Jesus Answers Your Dark Night of the Soul," Sojourners, April 4, 2016, https://sojo.net/articles/how-jesus-answers-your-dark-night-soul.

CHAPTER 8 | BRING JOY

1. *Cambridge Dictionary*, "sadness," accessed February 23, 2024, https://dictionary.cambridge.org/us/dictionary/english/sadness.
2. *Merriam-Webster Dictionary*, "sad," accessed February 23, 2024, www.merriam-webster.com/dictionary/sad.
3. Centers for Disease Control and Prevention, "National Center for Health Statistics FastStats: Depression," reviewed October 25, 2024, https://www.cdc.gov/nchs/fastats/depression.htm.
4. Philip Irving Mitchell, "A Biblical Model of Personhood," Dallas Baptist University, accessed June 3, 2025, https://www.dbu.edu/mitchell/early-modern-resources/personho.html.
5. David Brooks, "The Difference Between Happiness and Joy," *New York Times*, May 7, 2019, www.nytimes.com/2019/05/07/opinion/happiness-joy-emotion.html.
6. BibleProject, "The Seven Festivals," November 18, 2019, https://bibleproject.com/podcast/seven-festivals; and "What Are the Different Jewish Festivals in the Bible?" GotQuestions.org, accessed May 15, 2025, www.gotquestions.org/Jewish-festivals.html.
7. "How Does Compound Interest Work?" Securian Financial, accessed May 15, 2025, www.securian.com/insights-tools/articles/how-compound-interest-works.html.
8. As shared in "Keeping Your Joy Alive," a sermon by Nathan Johnson, Griffith Baptist Church, Griffith, Indiana, August 3, 2008, https://sermoncentral.com/sermons/keeping-your-joy-alive-nathan-johnson-sermon-on-heart-125182.

CHAPTER 9 | SEEK TO COMFORT

1. "Ramstein Air Base Commemorates Victims of Airshow Tragedy," Allied Air Command, accessed July 29, 2024, https://ac.nato.int/archive/2018/ramstein-air-base-commemorates-victims-of-airshow-tragedy.

2. Dave Trojan, "C-5 Galaxy Crash Ramstein AB Germany," AirCraftWrecks.com, February 2020, www.aircraftwrecks.com/pages/dave%20trojan%20mrp/C-5%20crash%20Ramstein%20Germany.pdf.
3. "Capt. Bradley Schuldt; Died in Air Force Crash," *Chicago Tribune*, updated August 10, 2021, https://www.chicagotribune.com/1990/08/31/capt-bradley-schuldt-died-in-air-force-crash.
4. "Capt. Bradley Schuldt," *Chicago Tribune*, August 10, 2021.
5. This chapter's trajectory was largely influenced by Harry's sermon on consolation. "VIA: Becoming an Instrument of Peace," sermon by Harry Li, recorded March 3, 2024, Mosaic Church of Central Arkansas, MosaicChurchMedia, YouTube, 27 min., 46 sec., www.youtube.com/watch?v=6J7LfNLzjXQ.
6. "VIA," sermon by Harry Li, March 3, 2024.
7. "VIA," sermon by Harry Li, March 3, 2024.
8. *Merriam-Webster Dictionary*, "console," accessed July 29, 2024, https://www.merriam-webster.com/dictionary/console.
9. Ferdinand Mount, "The Monster We Hate to Love," *The Spectator*, November 11, 2006, https://www.spectator.co.uk/article/the-monster-we-hate-to-love.
10. Steve Brawner, "Commentary: Mom Says Grief a Lifetime Journey," *Southwest Times Record*, updated December 23, 2012, https://www.swtimes.com/story/opinion/2012/12/23/commentary-mom-says-grief-lifetime/26319827007.
11. Brawner, "Commentary: Mom Says Grief."

CHAPTER 10 | TRY TO UNDERSTAND

1. Ironically, just a few weeks prior to the writing of this chapter, the owners of the building approached us again. While we've not yet come to terms, I continue praying one day we can acquire it for these purposes.
2. Blue Letter Bible, "Lexicon: Strong's H998—*bînâ*," accessed July 18, 2024, www.blueletterbible.org/lexicon/h998/niv/wlc/0-1.
3. These insights were shared with our congregation during a message on the topic of understanding. See "VIA: Becoming an Instrument of Peace," sermon by Lawrence Hicks, recorded March 10, 2024, Mosaic Church of Central Arkansas, MosaicChurchMedia, YouTube, https://www.youtube.com/watch?v=0uqEeHwdohg.
4. "With the Freedom of Speech, the Responsibility to Listen," Ford Foundation, accessed July 17, 2024, www.fordfoundation.org/news-and-stories/big-ideas/with-four-freedoms-four-responsibilities/with-the-freedom-of-speech-the-responsibility-to-listen.
5. "With Freedom of Speech," Ford Foundation.
6. "With Freedom of Speech," Ford Foundation.
7. The Kingdom's mission is to see others reconciled to God through faith in Jesus Christ, and to one another in the church beyond the distinctions of this

world that otherwise divide us along the lines of color, class, or culture, so that together we can advance a credible gospel (Ephesians 2:8-22).

8. Roya Nikkhah, "Prince William: Diana Inspires Me More than Ever to End Homelessness," *The Times*, October 26, 2024, https://www.thetimes.com/uk/royal-family/article/prince-william-diana-inspires-me-more-than-ever-to-end-homelessness-td956j0w8.
9. Nikkhah, "Prince William."
10. The Royal Family, "The Prince of Wales Visits Sheffield with Homewards," Royal.UK, March 19, 2024, https://www.royal.uk/news-and-activity/2024-03-19/the-prince-of-wales-visits-sheffield-with-homewards.
11. Brodie Owen, "Nansledan: Prince William to Build Homes for Homeless on Duchy Land," BBC News, February 18, 2024, https://www.bbc.com/news/uk-england-cornwall-68330944.
12. Lauren Collins, "Concerns Over 2500 Home Duchy Development," BBC News, April 9, 2024, https://www.bbc.com/news/articles/cjq527g2ldzo.
13. Space Center Houston, "Science in Action: Newton's Third Law of Motion," February 22, 2022, https://spacecenter.org/science-in-action-newtons-third-law-of-motion.
14. The quote "The definition of *insanity* is doing the same thing over and over again and expecting different results" is widely misattributed to Albert Einstein. However, there is no substantive evidence that Einstein ever said or wrote this phrase. According to an article on History.com, the earliest known usage of this quote appeared in a 1981 Narcotics Anonymous pamphlet, and it was later popularized by author Rita Mae Brown in her 1983 novel *Sudden Death*. The misattribution to Einstein seems to have emerged years after his death. Sarah Pruitt, "Here Are 6 Things Albert Einstein Never Said," History.com, updated May 28, 2025, www.history.com/articles/here-are-6-things-albert-einstein-never-said.
15. Mark DeYmaz, "7 Guiding Principles for Advancing Peace," *Outreach* magazine, July 6, 2023, https://outreachmagazine.com/features/multiethnic/69919-7-guiding-principles-for-advancing-peace.html.

CHAPTER 11 | PURPOSE TO LOVE

1. Kendra Cherry, "Do You Know What Love Really Is?" Verywell Mind, updated May 6, 2024, www.verywellmind.com/what-is-love-2795343.
2. Scott Edwards, "Love and the Brain," Harvard Medical School, accessed March 15, 2024, https://hms.harvard.edu/news-events/publications-archive/brain/love-brain.
3. Melissa and Scott Symington, "Understanding 'Agape Love' as the Highest Form of Intimacy," *RelateStrong* (blog), October 11, 2018, https://boonecenter.pepperdine.edu/blog/posts/understanding-agape-love.htm.

4. Bruce Hurt, "Love—Phileo (Greek Word Study)," Precept Austin, updated August 22, 2016, www.preceptaustin.org/love-phileo.
5. My friend Dr. John M. Perkins taught me this years ago. Dr. Perkins is a renowned author and teacher on issues of racial reconciliation, leadership, and community development. Learn more at https://www.johnmperkins.com.
6. In case you're wondering, I played third base as a freshman at Mesa Community College, in Mesa, AZ (1979–1980), and then for three years at Liberty University in Lynchburg, VA (1981–1983).
7. The account of Lilias Trotter's was largely derived from the 2015 documentary file *Many Beautiful Things*, written and directed by Laura Waters Hinson. See https://www.laurawatershinson.com/many-beautiful-things.

CHAPTER 12 | GIVE

1. "First flown in 1935, the Douglas DC-3 became the most successful airliner in the formative years of air transportation, and was the first to fly profitably without government subsidy. More than 13,000 DC-3s, both civil and military versions, U.S. and foreign built, were produced. Many are still flying." See "Douglas DC-3," National Air and Space Museum, accessed June 15, 2025, https://airandspace.si.edu/collection-objects/douglas-dc-3/nasm_A19530075000.
2. Read the entire creed in "The Full Text of the Nicene Creed," Bibles.net, accessed August 22, 2025, https://www.bibles.net/the-full-text-of-the-nicene-creed. See also https://christianhistoryinstitute.org/magazine/article/which-creed-is-which for a little history of the Nicene Creed.
3. Paul provides a synopsis of the gifts of security, significance, and salvation God has given to us via faith in Jesus Christ in Ephesians 1:3-11.
4. As exemplified in Christ's encounter with the woman at a well in the Samaritan town of Sychar (John 4:1-42). Learn more about historical animosities between Jews and Samaritans at Pat McCloskey, "The Rift Between Jews and Samaritans," Franciscan Media, May 16, 2020, https://www.franciscanmedia.org/ask-a-franciscan/the-rift-between-jews-and-samaritans.
5. This section is largely influenced by a sermon on giving by Dr. Harry Li. See "VIA: Becoming an Instrument of Peace," sermon by Harry Li, recorded March 23, 2024, Mosaic Church of Central Arkansas, MosaicChurchMedia, YouTube, 24 min., 59 sec., www.youtube.com/watch?v=WUsuvAs8aLw&t=472s.
6. Li, "VIA," March 23, 2024.
7. Thomas O. Chisholm, "Great Is Thy Faithfulness," 1923. Public domain.

CHAPTER 13 | PARDON

1. Vatican City is a landlocked sovereign country, an enclave within Rome, Italy.
2. Lance Morrow, "Pope John Paul II Forgives His Would-Be Assassin," *Time*, January 19, 1984, https://content.time.com/time/subscriber/article/0,33009,952295,00.html.

3. Morrow, "Pope John Paul II Forgives," *Time*, January 19, 1984.
4. *Merriam-Webster Dictionary*, "forgive," accessed March 30, 2024, www.merriam-webster.com/dictionary/forgive.
5. *Merriam-Webster Dictionary*, "pardon," accessed March 30, 2024, www.merriam-webster.com/dictionary/pardon.
6. These men were thieves or robbers (Mark 15:27, KJV, ESV). "Though people tend to use the terms interchangeably today, there seems to be a distinction between thieves (*κλέπται, kleptai*) and robbers (*λησταί, leistai*) in the ancient world. Thieves and burglars break into places and steal valuables, but *robbery often refers to a violent crime in antiquity.* Robbers, bandits, and raiders do not merely snatch goods; rather, they seize them by force after brutalizing or murdering their victims. The book of [Sirach] 36:31 (second century BCE) speaks of a 'nimble *thief* (*ληστής, leisteis*)' who is hard to catch because he skips from city to city. The Letter of Jeremiah [6:57] (second century BCE) uses the same term when it mentions idols of deities that cannot defend their temples from plunderers." Pinchas Shir, "Who Were the Two Thieves?," Israel Bible Center, May 15, 2023, https://weekly.israelbiblecenter.com/who-were-the-two-thieves. (*Note:* Here I have corrected Shir's mistaken attribution of Baruch 36:31 to *Sirach* 36:31 as well as his mistaken citation of the Letter of Jeremiah 6:14 to 6:57. In my view, these missteps do not diminish his understanding of the words in question.)
7. William Lane Craig, "Divine Forgiveness as Legal Pardon," Reasonable Faith, accessed May 15, 2025, www.reasonablefaith.org/writings/scholarly-writings/christian-doctrines/divine-forgiveness-as-legal-pardon.
8. Blue Letter Bible, "Lexicon: Strong's H7368—*rāḥaq*," accessed March 30, 2024, www.blueletterbible.org/lexicon/h7368/esv/wlc/0-1.
9. Theologian Wayne Grudem explains that "in the same way in which Adam's sins were imputed to us, so God *imputed* our sins to Christ; that is, he *thought of them as belonging to Christ* and, since God is the ultimate judge and definer of what really is in the universe, when God thought of our sins as belonging to Christ then in fact they actually did belong to Christ. This does not mean that God thought that Christ had himself committed the sins, or that Christ himself actually had a sinful nature, but rather that the guilt for our sins (that is, the liability to punishment) was thought of by God as belonging to Christ rather than to us." Wayne Grudem, *Systematic Theology: An Introduction to Biblical Doctrine* (Zondervan, 1994), 497.
10. 1 John 1:9; Hebrews 10:10.
11. Ephesians 2:8.
12. 2 Corinthians 5:21.
13. Though we are no longer enslaved by Sin (i.e., our Sin nature), at times we still sin. In part, this is because we have a history, have developed habits, are surrounded by, and are enticed to sin. When we give in to sin, we act

in accordance with our fleshly desires and not the Spirit who will otherwise produce good fruit in our lives (Galatians 5). As the redeemed of Christ, we have a choice in the matter; by the Holy Spirit within, we can reject sin. More than that, by way of repentance after the fact, we can renew and restore our walk with him.

14. See Corrie ten Boom with Jamie Buckingham, *Tramp for the Lord* (CLC Publications, 1974), 55–57.
15. Ten Boom, *Tramp*, 55–57.
16. Desmond Tutu and Mpho Tutu, "Desmond Tutu: On Why We Forgive," DailyGood.org, May 6, 2024, www.dailygood.org/story/688/desmond-tutu-on-why-we-forgive-desmond-tutu-and-mpho-tutu.
17. "This Day in History: Nelson Mandela Released from Prison," History.com, updated March 2, 2025, www.history.com/this-day-in-history/nelson-mandela-released-from-prison.
18. Alessandro Gisotti, "Forgiveness Liberates the Soul and Removes Fear," L'osservatore Romano, July 22, 2022, https://www.osservatoreromano.va/en/news/2022-07/ing-029/forgiveness-liberates-the-soul-and-removes-fear.html.
19. Gisotti, "Forgiveness Liberates," L'osservatore Romano, July 22, 2022.

CHAPTER 14 | FLOURISH

1. Sally Bavin, "Life Cycle of a Plant: Seeds, Shoots and Roots," WoodlandTrust.org, March 2, 2021, https://www.woodlandtrust.org.uk/blog/2021/03/plant-life-cycle-seeds-shoots-roots.
2. Blue Letter Bible, "Lexicon: Strong's G5091—*timaō*," accessed May 15, 2025, https://www.blueletterbible.org/lexicon/g5091/nasb20/mgnt/0-1.

About the Author

Mark DeYmaz is a thought-leading author, pastor, and recognized champion of the multiethnic church movement. Before planting the Mosaic Church of Central Arkansas in 2001, where he continues to serve as directional leader, he spent eighteen years in student ministry.

In 2004, Mark cofounded the Mosaix Global Network, where he serves as executive director and convener of the triennial Mosaix Conference. In 2008, he launched Vine and Village, a nonprofit dedicated to advancing the common good in Little Rock's University District, where he remains actively involved as a board member.

He holds an MA in exegetical theology from Western Seminary and a DMin from Phoenix Seminary. Mark also serves as an adjunct professor at Wheaton College, where he established the Mosaix Institute at the Wheaton College Billy Graham Center.

Since 2010, Mark has been a contributing editor for *Outreach* magazine. He is the author of eight books, including the groundbreaking works *Building a Healthy Multi-Ethnic Church* and (with Harry Li) *The Coming Revolution in Church Economics.*

Mark and his wife, Linda, have been married nearly forty years and live in Little Rock, Arkansas, near their four adult children and six grandchildren.